practical CLASSICS

ON

MGB

RESTORATION

Reprinted from
Practical Classics magazine

ISBN 0 946489 42 4

Published by
Brooklands Books with the permission of *Practical Classics*
Printed in Hong Kong

practical CLASSICS

Titles in this series

PRACTICAL CLASSICS ON AUSTIN A40 RESTORATION
PRACTICAL CLASSICS ON LAND ROVER RESTORATION
PRACTICAL CLASSICS ON METALWORKING IN RESTORATION
PRACTICAL CLASSICS ON MIDGET/SPRITE RESTORATION
PRACTICAL CLASSICS ON MINI COOPER RESTORATION
PRACTICAL CLASSICS ON MGB RESTORATION
PRACTICAL CLASSICS ON MORRIS MINOR RESTORATION
PRACTICAL CLASSICS ON SUNBEAM RAPIER RESTORATION
PRACTICAL CLASSICS ON TRIUMPH HERALD/VITESSE
PRACTICAL CLASSICS ON TRIUMPH SPITFIRE RESTORATION
PRACTICAL CLASSICS ON VW BEETLE RESTORATION
PRACTICAL CLASSICS ON 1930S CAR RESTORATION

Titles in preparation will cover:
VW Beetle, MG Midget

Distributed by:

Brooklands Book Distribution Ltd.,
Holmerise, Seven Hills Road,
Cobham, Surrey KT11 1ES,
England.   Tel: 09326 5051

Motorbooks International,
Osceola,
Wisconsin 54020 U.S.A.
Tel: 715 294 3345

practical CLASSICS

CONTENTS

INTRODUCTION

The MGB is one of Britain's most popular sports cars, even though it has been out of production for quite a few years. And justifiably too, because it represents a blend of looks, performance and praticality that makes it unique. So it should come as no surprise that *Practical Classics* has paid so much attention to the good old 'B', coverage which finally included the adoption of a chrome-bumper roadster as a 'Project Car', rebuilt over a period of two years by John Hill's MGB Centre at Redditch.

This initially decrepit two-seater was brought up to near-new condition by a series of operations which included a total body rebuild, suspension, brakes and steering overhaul, trimming, painting, and the replacement of all chrome parts. Subsequently, the original engine and gearbox were replaced by Gold Seal units. All these tasks were followed by the camera in great detail, and, with additional MGB material included from earlier and later issues of *Practical Classics,* are now brought together in this one volume. So — if you want to know how to replace a rusty sill, fit new kingpins, or even change a rubber-bumper car into a chrome-bumper one (or vice versa!), read on. It's all here!

Introducing the MGB Restoration!

STARTS THIS MONTH

We're following the total rebuild of an MGB, covering all the major jobs an owner is likely to encounter. Part One of the most detailed MGB analysis ever!

The MGB left production with something of a whimper, and the last models will probably not be remembered as the greatest what with the raised ride height taking the edge off its handling and the clumsy black bumpers degrading its looks — in many people's opinions anyway. But as about the last mass-produced, traditional British open sports car it was still much loved both here and abroad, and now that you can no longer buy a new one, it must make sense to look after the ones which are left, so long as you don't pick one that's too far gone.

To show exactly what is involved in the reconditioning of an MGB — body, mechanics and trim — over the next few months we will be following the total restoration of a typical mid-range car, a 1971 chrome bumper roadster, at John Hill's MGB Centre at Redditch. The Centre doesn't normally take on restoration jobs — parts are its main concern — but there's very little that John Hill doesn't know about putting Bs together so here's your chance to capture some of his expertise for yourself. You may not want or

need to undertake the whole works as we're going to do, but it's a sure bet that if you run an MGB of any description that's more than a few years old, you'll have to do *some* of the jobs we'll be looking at; so start reading here!

In the first paragraph we warned about choosing a 'goner' — you can waste an awful lot of time and money on a car which is too decayed structurally, so the first step in the restoration is to make sure that your car (or the one you're about to buy) is a practical proposition; and by now, even '73/'74 cars can

PROJECT CAR

5

Introducing the MGB Restoration!

Rust on the outer panels usually betrays itself — these are typical front wing corrosion spots on a 'B' around head and side lights. Front valance usually holes too.

Rear wheel arch rusts where inner wing joins it; damage is usually confined to perimeter of the panel, below the waistline moulding.

Look inside the front wheel arch for holes in the closing panel behind the front wheel.

Outer sills are almost certain to have holed, at spots like this and underneath where they meet the floor. Don't be fooled by 'over sills' which merely cover rotten originals — and proper sill replacement involves wing surgery as we will be seeing later.

be too rough to be worth the effort if they've led a hard life.

In fact it is a fairly safe bet to say that virtually all pre-1977 cars have rust in them to some degree, unless they've been properly rustproofed internally. This will be evident from blisters in the paintwork (or actual holes in earlier, unrepaired cars) in the usual places — round the head and sidelights, lower half of the front wings, bottoms of sills, all around the rear wheel arch, and in the rear valance. These are usually self-evident so long as they haven't been covered up with filler and new paint — use a small magnet if you can't detect the filler by running your hand over the danger areas — and are to be expected unless you're paying a fortune and buying an exceptional example. So the real task is to determine whether or not the rust has attacked the really vital parts of

the structure as opposed to the comparatively easy-to-replace outer panels.

Home in, therefore, on the inner sill walls as shown in our diagram. These are covered by rubber matting and in very bad examples the rot can be felt right through this if you press it. But normally you need to partially peel the rubber back where the sill meets the floor inside the car, and tap the wall with some sort of blunt instrument. If there's a nice hollow sound you're okay — but if the rot is well advanced think carefully about that particular car!

Having evaluated your car, you can get a fair idea of the cost and effort involved by listing the parts which need to be replaced or repaired, researching the prices of the replacement bits, and deciding what, if any, outside labour you will have to employ. Most cars have their good points — maybe the previous owner fitted an authentic reconditioned engine and box, or perhaps the car has an excellent interior. Beware of the car which needs drastic attention in *every* department — it may be a lot cheaper to purchase a better example and start on that.

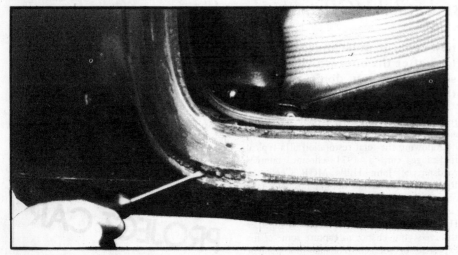

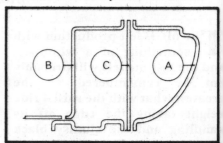

Diagram showing the construction of the MGB's sill in cross-section. Condition of outer sill (A) will be obvious so the most important check is (B), which means pulling back the rubber which is glued to it. Sill diaphragm (C) can be assumed to have rusted if (A) or (B) are, and we'll be covering replacement of all three.

6

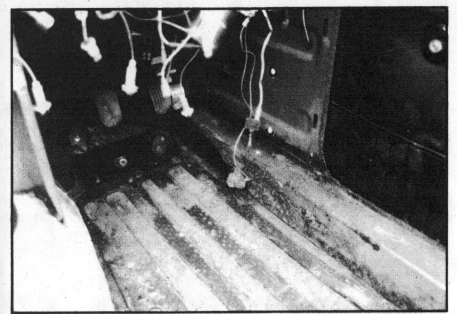

This is more serious — and it's essential to look behind the rubber covering the inner sill wall in order to check for rot like this, which if extensive may mean the car is not worth rebuilding.

STARTING THE REBUILD

If you're embarking on a full-scale restoration then you don't need to keep the car mobile, as is possible if just new front wing sections are, for example to be fitted. With our MGB it was a case of total strip-down, and the first things to come out effect safety — the batteries from behind the seats, and the fuel tank.

The former are no problem, but extracting

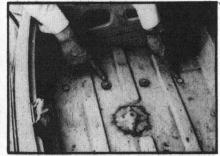

Petrol tank is accessible through boot (this is a GT), with these topmost bolts often being the most difficult to deal with.

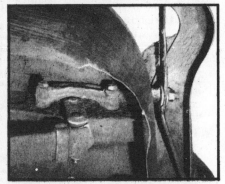

This is the curved bracket mounted above the rear spring shackle from which the bumper irons (right) have to be unbolted. It's no good unbolting it from the chassis rail before doing this because it won't go through the hole in the valance.

the petrol tank can produce bad language. It is held in place by studs and nuts underneath, and by bolts in captive nuts on top, accessible from the boot floor. Funnily enough it is these top ones which cause the trouble, as the bolts either round off or the captive nuts into which they go break free and revolve, so they should be tackled first. John has a set procedure for stubborn bolts — if they don't come free almost at once, drill an 1/8-inch pilot hole in the bolt head, then a larger hole sufficient to break the head off. If this is resorted to immediately after sockets or spanners fail, then time and temper are saved. And it is *much* neater than the use if a chisel which can result in damage to the surrounding areas.

What about draining the petrol, you ask? Well, don't try undoing the drain plug because you'll probably tear the tank itself — anyway, not all Bs were fitted with them. The best

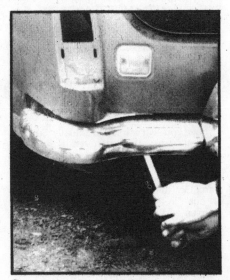

To get a ring spanner on the bolt on the end of the bracket, it may be necessary to also gently pull the bumper away from the body.

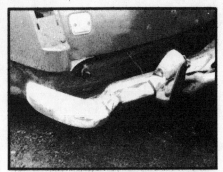

Rear bumper complete with irons can then be lifted away, leaving the bracket in place. It can now be unbolted if need be, as free from the bumper, it can be withdrawn forwards.

method is to either drive the car until the tank's more or less empty, or to undo a fuel line and allow the SU pump to discharge the contents into a suitable container.

One good reason for taking the tank out at an early stage is that removing the rear bumper is usually a bit of a struggle and heat may be needed on the bolts. You can forget about the chrome bumper bolts themselves being co-operative — they always turn, says John, so the bumper blade has to be removed complete with the irons. These are bolted onto a bracket which is mounted on the chassis rails and protrudes through the rear valance — but as this bracket is curved and won't go through the valance, the irons have to be unbolted from it. This isn't easy either, as a ring spanner will often not get between bumper blade and valance for you to attack the nut involved. The only solution is to carefully lever the blade away from the body to give you access. So — reserve enough time for rear bumper removal!

Fortunately the front is easy by comparison, and comes away complete with brackets and irons. You can also remove the front valance while you're at it, by unbolting it from the captive nuts. Light units front and rear can be taken out, and you'll most likely find that the headlight bowls have rusted badly.

The front bumper is removed very simply by undoing the bolts holding the brackets to the car.

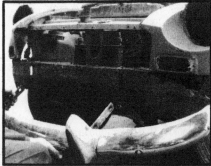

NEXT MONTH
Stripping out the interior, removing the dash, and removing front wings.

COMPANY HISTORY

The year was 1966 and the MBG GT was Abingdons latest model, John Hill was then still working for British Leyland serving an engineering apprenticeship. A bodyshell swop on what must have been the first insurance claim on an MGB GT prompted a build up of a complete new MGB using the damaged bodyshell. The resulting 'B' GT was re-registered in 1967 as OAB 479E and provided fast, reliable transport for many years while John completed his apprenticeship, commuting between Longbridge, Oxford and Abingdon plants.

The years 1966 to 1986 have seen rapid expansion due to the confidence shown in us by our MG customers.

From our modest start the Company has grown to one of the largest one-make sports car specialists. Two warehouses and land in Arthur Street provide storage for our new and secondhand spares, while additional properties provide our manufacturing facilities for panels, trim and machining — all to the most exacting standards imposed on us by British Motor Heritage. While stocks last we continue of course, to supply genuine Leyland components where possible.

We look forward to seeing you and your MGB!

THE MGB TIMES

Another "in-house" publication covering just about every topic of interest to the MGB owner. Whats more — "It's Free!" — make sure you are on the mailing list by sending SAE marked "The MGB Times".

This publication supercedes our very successful 'MG News' which was introduced during 1985. Packed with useful product information; helpful hints; bargains; special offers; clearance lines; letters; events; developments; news and history — but all only applicable to the MGB enthusiast!

"Body Building for 'B' Owners!!"

. . . have you ever wanted to actually 'See for Yourself' how to begin your rebuild/restoration?
Anyone can read plenty of books — but closer involvement is by far the best way to learn! Get the "MGB Times" for full details of our "in-house" MGB body building courses and other exclusive activities. We will keep you interested, entertained and involved with your MGB . . . "Long Live The MGB!"

PROJECTS

Over the past twenty years enthusiasts wi have seen the rebuild, restoration and re manufacture of many MGB's by the Centre Each project undertaken had a specific air in mind, for example the selection of repair and the final full restoration of the Practica Classics Red Roadster, which featured fo twenty-two issues of the magazine! Th story was then re-told in book form unde the title of 'MGB DIY Restoration Guid edited by Lindsay Porter.

Each year we have rebuilt, or even assemble from new parts, a complete MGB Centr Demonstrator (both GT's and Roadsters some of which have featured on our ow MG glamour calendars. These cars were a displayed at MG events up and down th country and finally sold off at the end c each season. Why not call in and see wha we are building for next season!

THE MGB CENTRE *Original*

TEL: REDDITCH (0527) 20880
ARTHUR STREET, REDDITCH,
WORCS. B98 8JY.

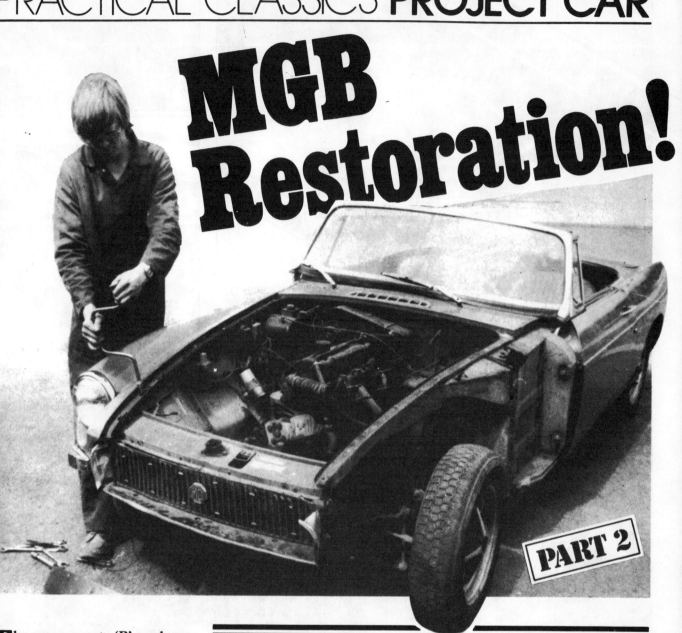

MGB Restoration!

PART 2

Our top-to-bottom restoration of an MGB roadster continues with stripping out the interior and dash, and taking off the front wings.

The average rusty 'B' needs new wings — it's as simple as that. Fitting new front wings is not particularly difficult and as you can still get the real thing in steel, it makes sense to forget about repairing the old ones if they're really bad and fit complete replacements instead, although bottom repair sections are available too. But first you've got to take the old wings off, and it's this — plus stripping the interior of the car — that we're covering in this episode with our 'Project Car' MGB.

John Hill, who runs the well-known MGB Centre at Redditch, has probably removed more MGB wings than you've had hot dinners, even though today the Centre concentrates on selling parts, rather than restoring cars. He reduced the *Practial Classics*

roadster to a wingless state in a very short period of time; this rate of progress comes from knowing the procedure, and anticipating the problems, so if you want your path similarly smoothed, read on.

As this particular car is, of course, being totally rebuilt, the interior was more completely stripped than is strictly necessary for just renewing the front wings. Not that there's an awful lot to it — the floor mats and battery cover are held in place by press studs, and after removing the seatbelt mountings on

each side of the transmission tunnel, the tunnel carpet (followed by the gearbox cover itself after removing the chrome gear retaining bezel) can be taken out. But first you should remove the seats.

Start by sliding the seats back as far as they

PROJECT CAR

MGB Restoration!

On removing the seats you should examine the floor for rust.

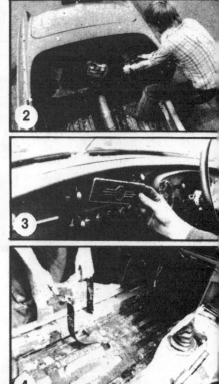

Arrows show the positions of the wing mounting bolts; screen pillar slots through top of wing on roadsters and will be removed before the wing is finally released. The bolts which Dave of the MGB Centre is undoing are probably the easiest to get at and can be left until last.

go, and undo and withdraw the two 7/16 ins bolts which are revealed securing the front of the runners. Then slide the seats right forward and remove the two rear 7/16 ins bolts. The whole seat complete with runners can then be lifted free. John points out that it's worth noting that MGB seats are handed, and while

Always remove (or at least disconnect) the batteries before attempting any work on the dashboard.

Unclipping the radio blanking plate; heater control knobs on left also come off, and the control rods freed by undoing their securing nuts. When removing rev. counter (right) note that one of the two knurled nuts behind retain an earth lead.

If there is any doubt about the condition of the floor, you can strip out all the old sound-deadening material — especially if it seems to be absorbing moisture.

it is possible to refit them to the opposite sides, they can't be used along their full travel, and on reclining seats the handles foul.

On our car, the next step was to remove the rubber matting glued to the inner sill walls; if you are intending to restore your 'B' to complete originality (instead of fitting the specially tailored sill carpets which are now available) bear in mind that only the right-hand rubber sill coverings are obtainable new, so take great care in removing the left-hand one at least. All the old sound-deadening panels were stripped from the floor, so that this could be completely examined. We'll be dealing with trim replacement in a future instalment of course, covering everything from door casings to seats and what types and colours should go in what years of car.

Then came the dash; John says that it isn't completely necessary to take out the dash to remove the front wings, but it helps a lot and is amost obligatory when it comes to putting on the new wings. The procedure is somewhat more complex than the manual would have you believe, but the following should explain things.

First you have to remove the steering wheel, and then the steering column complete by disconnecting the universal joint and the bracket under the dashboard. Next remove the centre console (four Phillips screws), which

6

Close-up of the beading which goes between wing and top of scuttle; a new one comes with a replacement wing.

7

Typical rusty front valance exposed after bumper has been removed. The front bolt positions are arrowed again.

discloses two 7/16 ins AF bolts which have to come undone. Disconnect the water gauge sensor unit in the cylinder head and feed it carefully through the bulkhead; you can disconnect the oil pressure gauge at the gauge end, and the choke cable from the carburettors.

Now you take off the blanking plate which covers the slot for a radio (or the radio if you have one fitted), to expose one ½ ins AF nut which must be undone. Then using a long extension and socket, undo the other two ½ ins nuts situated at each end of the dashboard. Unlock the glovebox next and disconnect the supporting bracket at the back, after which you remove the rev. counter and speedometer (and its reset knob by undoing securing nut and disengaging it from its bracket) to gain access to the two 7/16 ins AF bolts positioned high up between these two instruments. Disconnect the heater control cable on the heater valve, lower the dashboard and make the final electrical disconnections. Lift the dashboard rearwards, then back and up so that you can lift it clear. A word of warning — don't attempt to mess around behind the dashboard at all before you've disconnected the battery itself, as this is the surest way to produce sparks and, perhaps, a very 'hot' MGB indeed! If you remember, last month's instalment mentioned removing the battery at the start of the rebuild.

Should your car be a roadster, then there's one other item that has to come out and that's the windscreen assembly; the two screws which secure the bottom bracket of the screen to the body must be removed, then the main securing bolts which are accessible after you've removed the dash as above. On the GT this extra job doesn't arise and you can get on with getting the wings off.

MGB front wings are not welded onto the body at any point, but secured entirely by bolts and some Phillips headed screws. The most obvious of the former are the line of ½

8

Dave holds the old wings rather like fishing trophies, after a successful removal operation.

ins AF bolts each side of the engine bay disclosed on opening the bonnet, but these should be left until you've tackled the more awkward ones — such as the three (½ ins AF) tucked up inside the front bulkhead, which is why you've removed the dash. On the offside, you need to take out the wiper motor as well.

These three bolts screw into captive nuts on the wing, and you're okay if the nuts don't spin in their cages. If they do, and the wing is scrap anyway, you can cut the wing on the outside and solve the problem that way, but if it isn't, you'll have to drill the bolt head off — a method which John Hill prefers to a cold chisel, as there is less chance of damaging other parts of the car by mistake. Drill a 1/8 ins pilot hole in the bolt head, then open it out with a wider drill until it breaks off.

While you're groping about under the bulkhead, remove the trim panels (or scuttle

11

9

vehicles, rust and old under-sealant contribute to the problems. On very bad cars the wing may very well pull free at this point, having rotted right through, but you still have to get the screws out. Again, resorting to the drill is the best method.

The last sets of bolts are all at the front of the car. The bumper is removed as related last month, after which the three 7/16 ins bolts securing wing to under valance can be undone, while taking off the grille enables you to get at the two similar bolts which hold the wing to the inner wing. Then all you have to do is wind out the row of nuts down the side of the engine bay, and your wing should lift cleanly off.

Many owners are puzzled, John says, by the metal beading or fillet which is sandwiched between the front wing and the top of the scuttle just in front of the windscreen pillar, and it is this item which often leads people to believe that welding is involved with MGB front wings. In fact it's nothing to worry about and comes with your new steel wing.

If it were just a case of now being able to fit up your new wing, life would be easy. But in practice of course, the real work is only just beginning, as a rusty wing means a rusty sub-structure, notably the sill which extends forward to the wheel arch (which also suffers). The pictures show the typical trouble spots, and these will be tackled in future instalments. If you want to know in advance what parts are needed for this job, you can send for the MGB Centre's very detailed parts catalogue, issue no. 6, which besides bodywork also includes engine, suspension, brakes, electrical gear, wheels, accessories and virtually everything else you can think of which an MGB might need — even new bodyshells. It costs £1.50 including p&p. We shall, of course, be going over exactly what you need as we progress through the body rebuild, before we move onto the mechanical aspects of reviving a 'B'.

10

11

These views of what was revealed when the wings came away illustrate graphically what the average-to-poor MGB is like inside; front closing panel behind the wheels has decayed, mud on top of shelf formed by wheelarch/scuttle has caused large holes, and rust damage to sills, especially under door hinge pillar is very evident. These pictures also show the four vertical bolt holes adjacent to hinge pillar, and horizontal attachment points along top scuttle panel.

liners) on the outside of each footwell; you will then see the four 7/16 ins AF bolts which locate the back vertical edge of the wing adjacent to the door. These are probably the easiest of all to undo as they remain dry and rust doesn't get into them. They are, incidentally, the first to go in when the new wing is fitted, but we'll be coming to that stage at a later point.

The worst items of all to remove are the three Phillips headed screws at the bottom rear of the wing, along the sill line, and should be tackled at an early stage while you're still fresh! John says that these *never* undo even on near-new cars (they seem to have been put in by a very powerful air tool), and on older

---

NEXT MONTH

The intricacies of MGB sills as we cover their replacement step by step.

MGB Restoration!

PART 3

Replacing the sills — John Hill of the MGB Centre, Redditch, carries out this important job on our roadster.

If there's one bodywork job an owner is likely to tackle on his car, it's sill replacement. But what does sill replacement *really* entail, especially on an MGB?

To many people the sill is simply that nice curved bit under the door — just lop it off and bung on a new one, as sold by your local motor factors. But in reality there's a lot more to it than that, particularly on the MGB, and it's vital that the job is done correctly with all the right parts, otherwise you'll have wasted your time and maybe ended up with an unsafe car.

For a start, the outer bit which everybody sees is little more than a cover plate; as can be seen from the diagram, behind it is a box section which adjoins the floor, and it is this which gives the car (especially the roadster)

most of its strength. And if that outer sill has rusted to the extent that holes have appeared, you can bet your life that the inner box section, and the sill floor, have suffered badly too. Furthermore, note that the outer sill does a lot more than fill the gap under the door — it extends right inside both the front and rear wings.

This means that to do the job properly, the front wing has to come off (as described last month) and the bottom of the rear wing cut away (which can also be done with the front wing to save taking it off; like the rear wing it's normally rusty at this point anyway). The next step, says John, is to assemble the parts you think you'll need, and the normal minimum are: outer sill, diaphragm (i.e. the internal 'middle wall'), rear wing repair panel, and new front wing or repair panel. You'll need the last

mentioned from the start, in order to mark out the area of the wings to be cut for access to the sill inside.

Next, check the door gap to see whether, due to advanced rot, your car has a tendency to sag in the middle. Assuming that the hinges are not badly worn, the door should have an even gap all round, and should be level with the body at the top and waistline moulding. If the shell has sagged a little, it can very carefully be opened up to the correct width by some judicious jacking from the centre of the car, via a strong board on the floor pan to

PROJECT CAR

MGB Restoration!

This is how we left our MGB last month, with the front wings off; note how the sill extends inside the wing and attaches to the bulkhead sides.

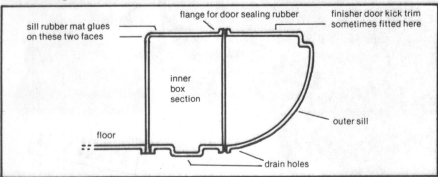

Diagram showing the construction of the MGB's sill in cross-section. Much more to it than just a bit under the door!

These are the basic repair panels used for a thorough job. New jacking point (and there's also an internal reinforcement for this) is shown along with front and rear wing repair sections, outer sill, internal wall, and sill floor.

Wing repair panels are offered up and the old wings scribed where repair sections end; cut is made about ½-inch under line. Outer sill is tackled by chiselling through top adjacent to flange as shown.

Hacksaw is then used to cut through sill (in toward car) at the point where sill appears to join wing in door aperture. This centre section can then be lifted away to reveal inner diaphragm.

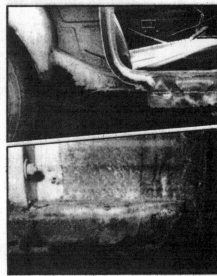

Those remaining bits of outer sill (formerly hidden by the wings) are removed next; a chisel, cutting disc or saw can be employed, but flame cutting is a poor alternative.

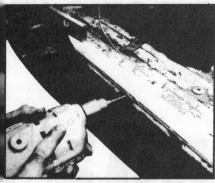

The flange of the old outer sill, and the inner wall or diaphragm, are removed by drilling the spot-welds holding them onto the right-angled inner sill wall.

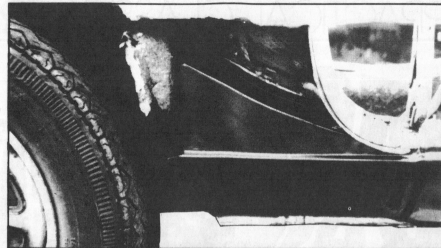

As the spot welds are disposed of, the diaphragm can be peeled off; flange behind may need dressing afterwards. Note triangular reinforcement bracket for jacking point which often needs to be replaced as well.

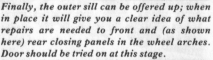

A fair amount of trimming is required to get the diaphragm to fit correctly, including under the door pillar.

Finally, the outer sill can be offered up; when in place it will give you a clear idea of what repairs are needed to front and (as shown here) rear closing panels in the wheel arches. Door should be tried on at this stage.

Again, self-tappers and clamps should be used as the outer sill is welded into place — and don't perform this operation until you're completely satisfied that the door fit is correct. Top flange may need dressing afterwards.

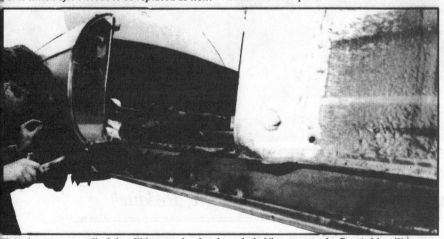

If the innermost wall of the sill box section has been holed(i.e. next to the floor) this will have to be repaired locally — complete replacement is unusual. Then after cleaning-up the remnants of the old sill floor, the new floor section is offered up, checked with the new diaphragm and outer sill, and then welded in position.

Diaphragm is offered up next, and clamped tightly in place.

Ideally the diaphragm is spot welded into position, but careful tack-welding is permissible otherwise. Ensure that panel is held in close contact with car through clamps and/or self tapping screws during any type of welding operation.

spread the load. Then before work commences, make sure that the car is supported on axle stands only where the shell is subject to input stresses from the wheels, that is under the rear axle and front suspension wishbones or mounting points. Additionally, supporting the floor gently on the side you're actually working (but not enough to affect the door gap unless it has to be altered) is a further guard against distortion which might occur as metal is removed.

The main sill replacement procedures are followed in the picture sequences. The main thing to remember is to double-check before doing any cutting or welding, and try the door fit at every relevant stage, because that and the outer sill line is what people are going to see. A 'B' (or 'C') repaired in this fashion is going to last a very long time, although do remember to paint sections with anti-rust paint before closing off, and injecting afterwards with anti-rust fluid when all welding has been completed.

NEXT MONTH
More bodywork repairs

MGB Restoration!

PART 4

This time we look at taking the MGB's engine out, with some expert advice by John Hill of the MGB Centre, Redditch.

This month we're back-tracking a little to cover the removal of the MGB engine and ancillaries, which most people would do for a complete rebuild, or if the power unit needs re-conditioning — though most things on the engine can be reached with it in the car, apart from actually taking out the crankshaft or replacing the main bearings.

Removing the power plant from an MGB presents no particular problems, and the main sequence of events is shown in the photographs. Note the method of removing the oil cooler complete which avoids damaging it; at the same time you can check that the feed pipes to the cooler haven't been chafing on the steering column UJ, which is not an unknown occurance, John says. Of course, oil and water should be drained early on in the proceedings, and the batteries (if not removed) disconnected.

You can, if you like, take the gearbox out as well, still attached to the engine, in which case you have to make all the gearbox disconnections too — gear lever, reversing light and speedometer drive included. Both engine and gearbox are then supported, the cross-member to frame bolts undone, the tie-bracket bolts undone, and the gearbox lowered so that it rests on the fixed chassis cross-member.

Having removed any stay rod or engine restraint, the cross-member is completely removed and the engine/gearbox assembly moved forward, then tilted up and out of the car.

The photographs accompanying (not all of the same car incidentally) show the engine coming out alone, which means that the starter motor has to come off followed by the bolts securing the bellhousing to the engine. The engine can then be drawn forward a few inches and then straight up and out; but take great care to avoid damaging the gearbox input shaft in the clutch which is rather susceptible to damage.

John Hill guides the engine clear of a roadster 'B', the engine being lifted on a rope sling positioned as seen. Whatever method you use, ensure that your tackle is strong and secure.

PROJECT CAR

MGB Restoration!

Assuming you've removed or at least dis-connected the batteries, taking off the bonnet by placing it on its prop and undoing the mounting bolts is the next step. Scribe or mark round hinges so that refitting can be done correctly.

Removing the carbs and aircleaners gives you more room to tackle the radiator mounting bolts so do this at an early stage. They can come off complete with cleaners or separately. Make the usual choke, throttle, return spring, and petrol feed disconnections, pull off the vacuum pipe and undo overflow pipes.

The shield is somewhat fragile and you should take this opportunity to examine it for damage.

Next you can move on to the radiators, both oil and water, which are situated as shown. Before removing the water radiator it's worth a glance to see if the gap at bottom is parallel — if not, it may be an indication of a front-end shunt at some time.

Don't attempt any disconnection at the oil cooler itself, which may well result in damage; instead, go to the engine and remove the pipes from the block. Two spanners are very often needed here to prevent the unions from turning.

The radiator diaphragm panel is unbolted next.

The oil cooler is then disconnected from the tray by undoing four 7/16 ins AF bolts, which allows you to lift both oil and water radiators, plus the diaphragm panel and pipework, out from the car.

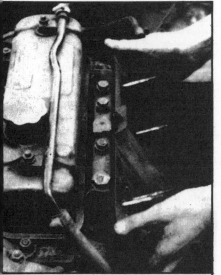

The heat shield follows the carbs, being pulled carefully off the studs.

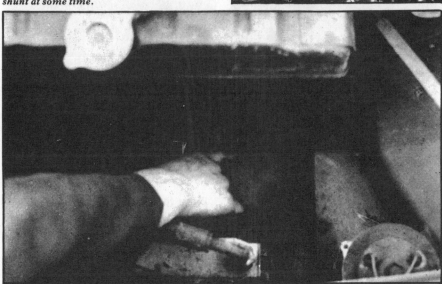

MGB ENGINE MOUNTINGS, ALL VERSIONS
Taken from the MGB Centre's catalogue.

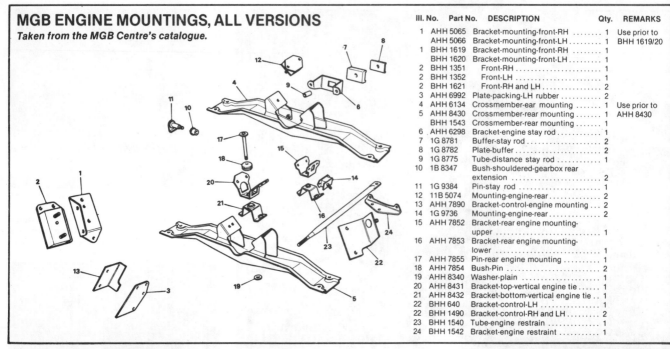

Ill. No.	Part No.	DESCRIPTION	Qty.	REMARKS
1	AHH 5065	Bracket-mounting-front-RH	1	Use prior to
	AHH 5066	Bracket-mounting-front-LH	1	BHH 1619/20
1	BHH 1619	Bracket-mounting-front-RH	1	
	BHH 1620	Bracket-mounting-front-LH	1	
2	BHH 1351	Front-RH	1	
2	BHH 1352	Front-LH	1	
2	BHH 1621	Front-RH and LH	2	
3	AHH 6992	Plate-packing-LH rubber	2	
4	AHH 6134	Crossmember-ear mounting	1	Use prior to
5	AHH 8430	Crossmember-rear mounting	1	AHH 8430
	BHH 1543	Crossmember-rear mounting	1	
6	AHH 6298	Bracket-engine stay rod	1	
7	1G 8781	Buffer-stay rod	2	
8	1G 8782	Plate-buffer	2	
9	1G 8775	Tube-distance stay rod	1	
10	1B 8347	Bush-shouldered-gearbox rear extension	2	
11	1G 9384	Pin-stay rod	1	
12	11B 5074	Mounting-engine-rear	2	
13	AHH 7890	Bracket-control-engine mounting	2	
14	1G 9736	Mounting-engine-rear	2	
15	AHH 7852	Bracket-rear engine mounting-upper	1	
16	AHH 7853	Bracket-rear engine mounting-lower	1	
17	AHH 7855	Pin-rear engine mounting	1	
18	AHH 7854	Bush-Pin	2	
19	AHH 8340	Washer-plain	1	
20	AHH 8431	Bracket-top-vertical engine tie	1	
21	AHH 8432	Bracket-bottom-vertical engine tie	1	
22	BHH 640	Bracket-control-LH	1	
22	BHH 1490	Bracket-control-RH and LH	2	
23	BHH 1540	Tube-engine restrain	1	
24	BHH 1542	Bracket-engine restraint	1	

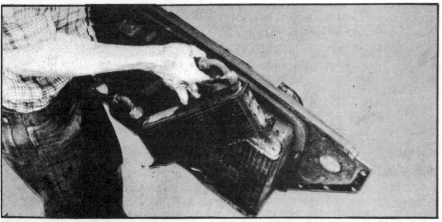

Unless work is needed on them, the whole cooling assembly can be put to one side and then replaced later as a complete unit, without having to be taken apart. It's a good time to give them a thorough clean though — but avoid getting water or emulsifier into the oil cooler.

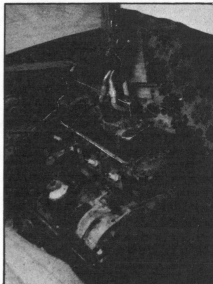

This engine is being lifted using a strongly made bracket which is attached using the rocker cover bolts.

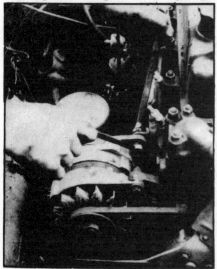

Removing the alternator or dynamo is optional, but does give you more room to get at the offside engine mounting bolts. The same applies to the exhaust manifold on the other side.

Tackling the nearside engine mounting bolts with two spanners having made all the engine/car disconnections.

Before you start heaving at the lifting tackle though, make sure you have made all the necessary disconnections, including water hoses (these can be sawn through for convenience if they are to be replaced anyway), electrical leads, control cable to water valve, and the oil and water gauge sender unit on top of the cylinder head. Make sure you don't damage the capilliary, John says, as if it gets broken the whole gauge will have to be swopped for a service exchange unit.

The usual warnings about lifting engines apply; power units are heavy lumps of metal and create havoc if they drop or otherwise get out of hand. Buy or hire suitable lifting gear and take things slowly. We'll be covering the re-conditioning of both the three- and five-bearing engines at a later stage.

NEXT MONTH
We return to the bodyshell of our 'B' and begin repairs to the front end.

MGB Restoration!

PART 5

Back to bodywork this month as we follow vital repairs to the front inner wings. Paul Skilleter reports from the MGB Centre at Redditch.

The front inner wing on a 'B' is, says John Hill, a potential problem area even with the latest cars off the line, because of the ledge which is formed by the 'box reinforcement' at the top of the wheelarch. As can be seen from the photographs, this is ideally positioned to collect mud thrown up by the wheel and, sandwiched by the top of the outer wing, the constant dampness rapidly produces rust. Eventually the top of the reinforcement box becomes holed, and water is allowed to enter the inner corners of the bulkhead so

spreading the rust even further afield.

The trouble is, all this goes on under the car's outer wing so nothing shows until it's too late — usually the full extent of the rot is only revealed when a front wing is actually taken off, whereupon the somewhat shocked owner discovers that he's in for a lot more repairs than he thought.... An instant inspection of the offside wheel arch in particular is extremely difficult on a right-hand drive car, because of the brake pedal assemblies and wiring harness which pass through this area. The best way of getting an idea of how much corrosion may be there is to look at the nearside, says John, which is without the complications mentioned. If that's badly

affected, you can bet that the offside isn't going to be any better.

You can also get an estimate of what the damage is by opening the bonnet and probing about from the inside. Otherwise, you have to take the front wheel off, reach up inside, clean the dirt from the ledge and try to feel any holes. On our 'B' of course all was revealed when the wings were taken off, which is essential anyway for actual repairs to this area. As you can see from the photographs, not only had the triangular reinforcement box gone but a good deal more besides, including the inner wall, wing mounting flange and the bracket which retains the voltage regulator; certainly a worse-than-average case for a '71 MGB, in John Hill's opinion.

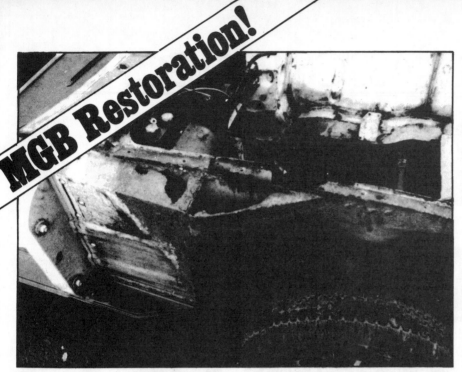

The damaged inner wing area to be repaired: note how virtually all the top horizontal surfaces are holed — or have disappeared completely! — and about 6 ins of wing mounting flange has gone.

Here the voltage regulator support panel, together with part of the wing mounting flange, is pushed back to allow the inner wing wall to be cut.

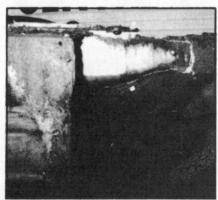

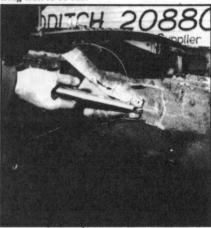

These are the parts which are available ex-stock for MGB inner wing repairs; everything else has to be made-up specially using mild steel sheeting.

This is how the inner wing looks with this panel removed; it is now possible to see the exact extent of the rot.

The area to be removed was marked out on sound metal below any rot, and then cut away using Monodex cutters — though you could use a padsaw after drilling holes to give a 'start'.

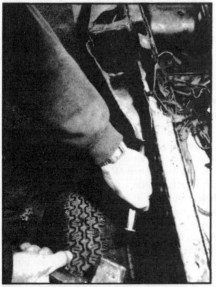

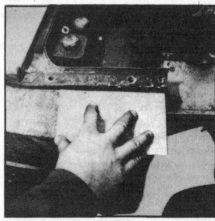

The triangular forward extension is the first part of the reinforcement box to be cut away, by drilling and chiselling the spot welds.

The new panel is offered up to determine the area it covers; this is the only major off-the-shelf replacement part available and adjacent repair sections will have to be made-up.

Next a flat section of sheet steel to cover the rot cut out from the rear part of the reinforcement box is cut to shape.

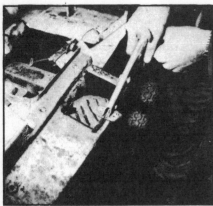

The rotten metal is then cut away with care.

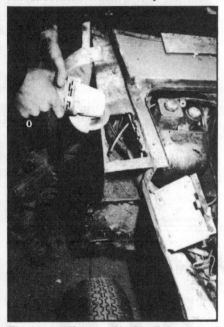

The surrounding metal is then finished ready for the patch to be put into position.

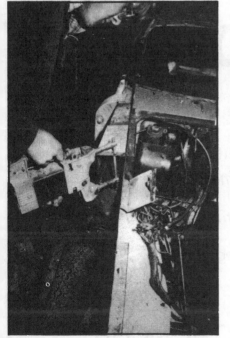

The patch, after final trimming, is spot-welded into position.

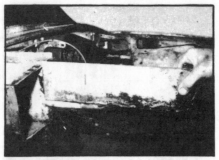

Another flat repair panel is made for the inner wing wall, which is cleaned up ready to accept it, after which the spot welder is brought to bear.

A further panel is made up for the outside of the box section as shown, and welded into place.

Now the two catalogued panels are spot welded together to form an assembly which is then offered up to the car.

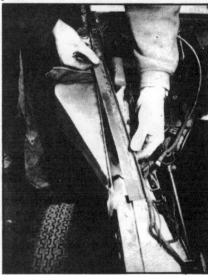

Here, the mud shield/box section assembly is spot-welded to the new section of inner wing; flange in the foreground is gas-welded into place.

A new length of wing-mounting flange is made-up and placed into position across the gap; the distance across the gap is then marked, and the new flange cut to fit exactly.

The new flange is welded to the repaired inner wing at intervals, and finally at each end. A complete 'run' is not attempted because of the risk of distortion.

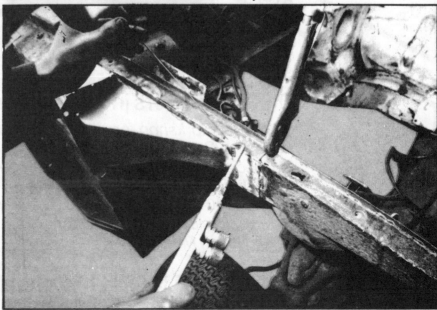

MGB Restoration!

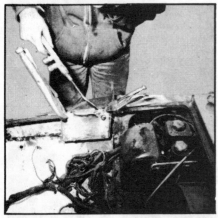

The voltage regulator support panel is repaired and then re-attached to the new flange.

The finished repair, all ready for painting — and additional protection such as under-body seal to prevent rust setting in again. Small rubber seal has yet to be fitted on top shoulder of mid-way flange.

However, even if your car turns out to be in a similar state, the job of putting it all back to rights is not a desperately hard one even for the home restorer. Only a couple of repair panels are available for this part of the car, but the additional ones are quite easily made from sheet steel without any special skill being needed. The sequence of operations is shown in the pictures — just observe the golden rule of planning the job carefully and do not go hacking metal out willy-nilly.

Our car was almost completely stripped out at this stage, but if you're working on a more complete example, don't go and set fire to the wiring harness which as mentioned runs along the right-hand (offside) front of the car — remove it or protect it against the flame. David Cartwright, who did most of the work for this job, used a spot-welder most of the time but normal gas welding can be employed instead — indeed it's essential in some places near the bulkhead, where the spot-welder's arms can't reach.

When the job is complete, it's a good idea to give everything a coat of anti-rust primer and to seal seams and overlaps with mastic. Finally, before the new front wings go on, a thick coat of under-sealant will help prevent this notorious trouble-spot from ever bothering your MGB again.

NEXT MONTH
Rear wing repairs

MGB Restoration!

PART 6

Our roadster has its rear wing put to rights — a detailed look at how it's done and with what. Paul Skilleter reports from the MGB Centre at Redditch.

We've already covered replacing the MGB's sills, and pointed out the big difference between a simple 'over sill' between the door pillars, and the genuine BL item which goes right behind both front and rear outer wings to join the inner wings. To fit the genuine article means cutting the rear wing whether it's good or not, and while this can be made good locally with the small repair panel illustrated, the normal elderly 'B' exhibits bad rust (and/or bad repairs) much further round the wheelarch.

So your first job is to ascertain the exact extent of the rot by poking and then stripping the metal; you can then judge which panel or panels are needed to put things right. There is now quite a selection to choose from and, says John Hill, their availability makes the repair of the wheelarch area a much easier job than it used to be when you had to fit a whole new rear wing — which apart from its initial cost, brought complications with aligning it to the

boot aperture on roadsters, and the tailgate area on GTs, because it extends right to these. You also have to do a lot more stripping out first. The complete rear wing (you can still get them, useful to put right accident damage or for an 'ultimate' rebuild) is shown along with a selection of part-panels in our heading picture.

What makes these repair panels practical and easy to fit is the design of the MGB wing as installed on the car. The key is that chrome body strip which runs along the side of the wing, where there's a step in the wing pressing. John says that it's virtually unknown for rust to extend up beyond this point, and the line makes an ideal joining point; so while the chrome strips and their metal studs initially encourage water to enter the rear wheel arch area and cause the rust, at least the styling and ribbing of the wing at this point help considerably the fitting of repair panels. The ribbing stiffens the area nicely, and when the chrome strip is replaced it helps to mask

any slight imperfections in the join. It's almost as if BMC designed it for this purpose, says John!

On our roadster, investigations showed that the entire lower rear wing from the chrome strip downwards needed replacing, and John chose to use two panels to replace the metal cut out. One advantage of using two panels is that the job can be tackled in stages and not so many clamps (or assistants!) are needed which is useful to the home rebuilder working with limited facilities. As the pictures show these two particular panels overlap considerably at the centre but it is not too difficult a job to achieve a butt join (having cut away the section of the front panel not needed) after everything has been lined up correctly.

PROJECT CAR

Our MGB before the job has been started — fairly typical rot all around the wheel arch, but note that it does not extend to or above the chrome strip.

Proper sill replacement means cutting out a piece of the rear wing at its front; this can be boxed-off afterwards using this small repair panel if the remainder of the wing is sound.

The sequence and method of cutting the rot out is detailed in the pictures, and while the 'shoulder' or ribbing along the rear wing does stiffen the panel, don't be tempted to use a chisel or you'll distort the area you're trying to preserve. This is perhaps the most tedious part of the exercise but don't attempt short cuts — use a hacksaw or non-distorting metal cutters, or an electric nibbler if you have one.

The lining-up part of the job is crucial to success, and it is particularly important to make sure that the door gap will be correct, which means re-fitting the door accurately to check on this. The panels are then self-tapped pop-rivetted to the car, overlapping the existing metal and trimmed off level with the shoulder adjacent to where the chrome strip fits. The panels can be secured with gas welding, or brazing with either gas or carbon arc torch, the pop rivets serving to locate the wing during these operations.

You may think it's odd that the rot evident in the inner wing has been ignored, but, says John, there's reason in that particular bit of apparent madness — the 'line' which most

Other, larger, repair panels are available for making good bigger areas of rust; the most popular is the one which covers the entire circumference of the wheel arch (centre).

needs to be right is the one that you see from outside the car, and if you attempt to rebuild the inner wing first, there is a real danger that it will alter the fit of the outer panels which, if not in contact with anything round the wheel arch, will otherwise lie naturally when offered up as we've described. So the inner wing is repaired afterwards, and of course we'll be covering that too along with a mention of

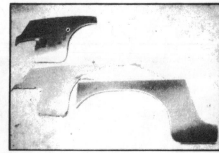

The rot in our 'B's wing extended almost to the rear valance which was more than the single largest panel covered. We therefore chose to use the two other (front and rear) repair panels, which together would cover the area left after cutting away the rusted section.

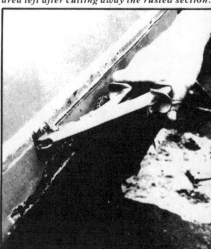

Cutting begins after removal of chrome strip, the cutter or hacksaw (not chisel) following a line which has been scribed ½ ins below the rivet holes.

This is a useful technique to separate wing from door shut pillar — an abrasive disc weakens the metal at the corners so that it can finally be chiselled away without distorting the pillar.

other repairs in that area. So it can be seen that this part of the 'B' is particularly amenable to repairs by the home enthusiast who works methodically and takes his time. You don't even have to possess welding or brazing equipment either, because you can do all your trimming and lining up, screw or pop rivet the fitted panels in place, and take the car to a professional welder for the finishing touches. □

The same procedure can be adopted to free outer wing from inner wing all round the wheelarch, and from the rear light platform — linishing then chiselling carefully.

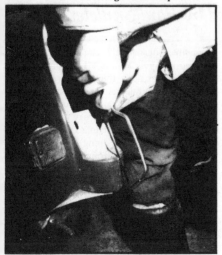

The hacksaw cut in the rear valance is dictated by the shape of the rear repair panel at this point — offer it up and scribe round it here, making sure to cut inboard of the line by at least ½ ins to allow a good overlap.

The hacksaw is again used directly under the rear light platform, to finally free the section being cut out.

Here the last cut is made and the metal comes away, revealing for the first time the true extent of rust damage to the inner wing.

The rust is certainly bad round the outer edges of the inner wing, but the metal is sound a few inches inwards. This view also shows the return flanges on the genuine BL full-length sill which are ideal for locating a new wheelarch or repair section.

The full area exposed by the surgery, showing the top cut ½ ins below the chrome strip line, and where the rear valance has been cut.

Next step is to prepare all edges, removing all traces of sealant or paint, and linishing to bright metal.

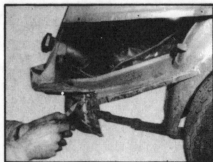

Any odd bits of metal left over from the cutting must be removed, and edges dressed with hammer and dolly if necessary to ensure they meet the repair panels accurately. Note that petrol tank is removed — only the filler pipe remains.

Starting from the rear of the car, the rear repair panel can be offered up for a trial fit, clamped in place and drilled for temporary location by self-tapping screws or pop rivets.

CONTINUED ON PAGE 31

MGB Restoration!

PART 7

*Our roadster gets the rear inner wing treatment —
more progress relayed by Paul Skilleter.*

A s with most cars, if an outer wing has rusted badly enough to warrant replacement, it's highly unlikely that the inner wing hidden behind has escaped undamaged. So it was with our MGB roadster, the corroded state of the inner wing all round the wheelarch being confirmed when the outer rear wing was repaired (as covered last month).

It might appear illogical to have replaced sections of the outer wing first, rather than making good the inner wing before hand. But the procedure which the MGB Centre adopts in this instance is not unusual, the theory being that the line of the *outer* wing is the one which you must get right (because it shows), and a repaired inner wing with the wrong contours could well put this out. So John Hill prefers to fit the outer wing repair sections and

only then turn his attention to the inner wing. Having the 'new' outer wing already in place certainly does give you an extra reference point which might not be there if the original outer wing had corroded away almost entirely.

Fitting the inner wing sections is detailed in the picture sequences; as with the fitting of all repair sections, it's important to offer the parts up carefully first before making any cuts in the metal, so that you know exactly what area is covered by the new panels. The inner wing repair sections as supplied by the MGB Centre cover a generous area which should easily bridge even the most extensive rust in this part of the car.

The existing inner wing should be cut so that there's about ¼-ins overlap with the repair sections, this cut being adjacent to a seam in the circumference of the inner wing at

this point. Alternatively, you can cut the inner wing so that you achieve a butt-join with the repair sections, but this of course involves much more accurate cutting and trimming.

The repair sections come in three parts, and this isn't just because you may only need one or two of these. The main reason is because fitting an entire inner wing 'half' would be very difficult in the confined space, but with three sections, starting with the front one, it is relatively simple. You should find that all three slot into the wheelarch very easily, with a minimum of shaping or trimming. Make sure that the centre repair section is pushed

PROJECT CAR

1

These are the three inner wing repair sections; they join at the edge of pressings.

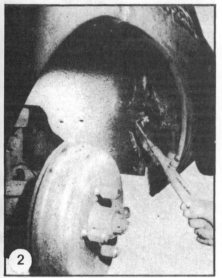

2

Having established where to cut, the rusted part of the old wheelarch can be removed; the MGB Centre used a gas torch but home restorers are probably better off using a cutting disc or pad saw.

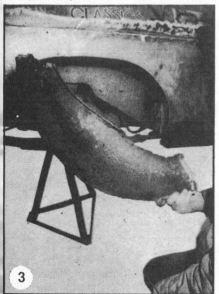

3

This is the old section of the inner wing being pulled free (upside down). If you are replacing the inner wing before the outer, spot-welds on wheelarch flanges adjacent to outer wing must also be broken.

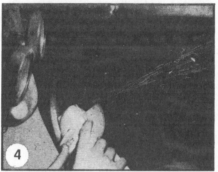

4

The edges of the remaining section of the inner wing are dressed flat and linished. If you are attempting a butt-weld with the new sections, considerable fitting work will be required at this stage.

5

What the inner wing looks like from inside the boot, with the rusted section removed (above). Flat panel immediately behind inner wing can be obtained as a separate item and fitted if the original has rusted, as shown (below).

6

The front inner wing repair panel is the first to be offered up; it should slot into place with little difficulty.

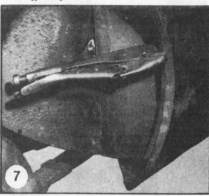

7

Note how the panel lines up with existing wheel arch at the bottom — this is why the front repair section is fitted first, because you have this referance point.

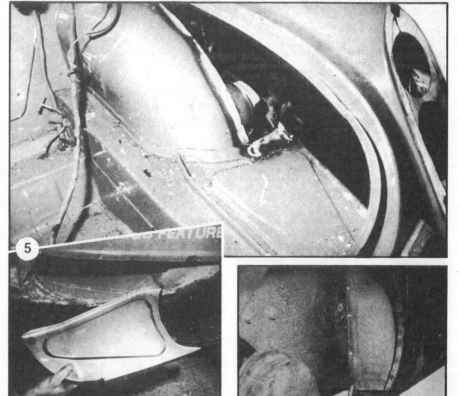

8

The new section must be held surely in position with clamps, and a line of self-tapping screws going into the overlapping wheelarch on the car.

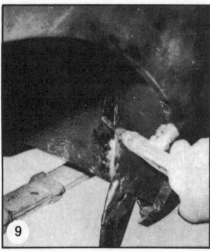

9

The welding torch can then be brought to bear, and the repair section tacked at intervals up round the wheelarch, and — with care — at separate spots along the outer flanges which overlap those of the outer wing.

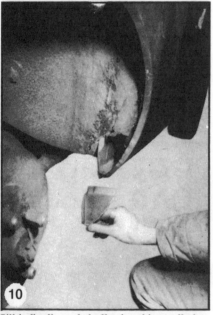

10

Sill is finally sealed off using this small plate (shown before inner wing repairs commenced).

11

Next, the centre repair section can be fitted up, the right-hand edge abutting that of the installed front section.

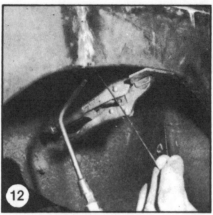

12

Clamped and self-tapped into place, the centre section is welded into position. Here the flanges are being welded.

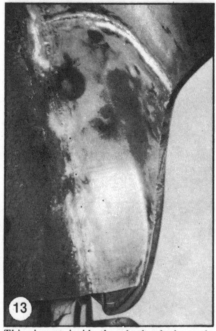

13

This view up inside the wheelarch shows the front repair section, and the butt-weld where it joins the front edge of the middle section. Holes left by self-tappers can be filled later.

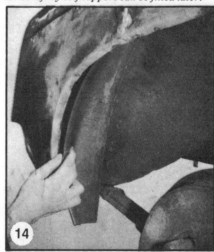

14

Finally, the rear section can be offered up. At the top it is butt-welded to the rear edge of the centre section. Note that at the bottom, it will correctly project downwards an inch or so compared to the inner wing itself.

15

The inner wing with the rear repair section now welded into position; self-tappers which secured it during welding have yet to be withdrawn.

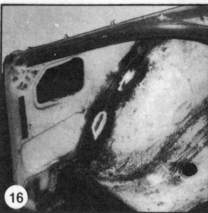

16

Front of the inner wing as viewed from inside the car, with welds showing through where front repair section has been welded. The overlap between welds can be sealed with braze.

well home though, as if it hasn't seated properly you may have trouble mating the rear section to it.

David Cartright, who did the work, secured the sections with short runs of weld at regular intervals, as indicated by the photographs. In between the welds, braze was later applied to seal off the metal, otherwise water would enter. A coating of mastic along all the seams, and where the inner and outer wing flanges meet all the way round the wheel arch, is not a bad idea either, to fill any pinholes and prevent water starting the rust again. □

NEXT MONTH

We turn to some mechanical aspects of the MGB as the rear wheel hub is dismantled for oil seal and half-shaft replacement.

MGB Half-shaft & Oil Seal Replacement

PART 8

This month we cover rear axle repairs as we follow a rear hub strip-down.

Oil seals are not everlasting and if you notice the tell-tail streaks of oil on the wheel, or find that your rear brakes are pulling to one side or not operating efficiently, the chances are the outer oil seal has gone on the axle. Or, the axle breather tube has become blocked and is causing pressurisation. More traumatically, half-shafts can break too, so here the dismantling procedure is followed on a later-type tube rear axle (as fitted to GT's from the start of production), at John Hill's MGB Centre, Redditch. The pictures show the sequence of events, and possibly you will be able to avoid having to locate special tools — though there's no point in struggling and you will certainly find life easier if you hire the correct ones from the start.

This strip-down also provides you with an opportunity for examining the brake linings, the condition of the rear brake cylinder, and it may well be worth fitting a seal kit at least to the cylinder if you have any doubts, while everything is in bits. So inspect it for rust — and if the pitting is deep, buy a new one, as a seal kit in that instance will only be a very temporary cure.

Another item to check is the splines on the hub, if a wire-wheeled car. Dry rust indicates previous lack of maintenance, and if the splines have become sharply 'pointed', then a new hub is desirable. Note that the wire-wheel hubs are handed, so make sure they go back on the same side of the car as they came from! The nearside hubs are righthand thread (unscrew anti-clockwise), the offside ones lefthand (unscrew clockwise). Note also that the axle shaft (hub) nut, secured by a split-pin, is righthand thread on both sides of the car.

PROJECT CAR

MGB Restoration!

1 *Slacken off the wheel nuts (or spinner), then jack the rear of the car up and place axle stands securely under the road springs.*

6 *Lever shoe off adjuster at top, then unclip the top pull-off spring. The brake shoes can then be removed. Brush off the brake dust but don't inhale it — the linings contain asbestos. Check the linings at this stage, and if they are oily or the rivets are near the surface, fit exchange shoes — in complete axle sets only.*

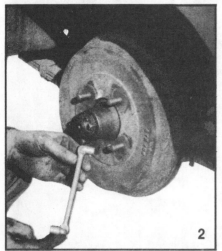

2 *Slacken off the brake adjusters (don't forget to release the handbrake) so that the shoes are clear of the drum and won't hinder its removal. Square adjuster is behind backplate.*

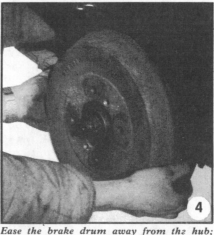

4 *Ease the brake drum away from the hub; sometimes a light tap from behind with a soft-headed hammer is necessary. The drum itself should be examined for scoring while it is off.*

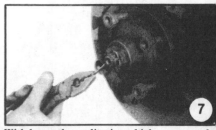

7 *Withdraw the split-pin which secures the castillated hub nut. Never re-use a split pin — ensure you have a new one to use when reassembling.*

3 *Remove the two Phillips-headed screws (nuts on wire-wheeled cars) which hold the drum to the hub; these are often chewed-up however, but giving the screw-driver a sharp tap first will often help to loosen them.*

5 *Using pliers, grip the retaining washer and press inwards against the spring, holding the steady-pin from behind the backplate. Turn the washer until it comes free of the pin's 'T' head. Make sure that you keep all the parts safely.*

8 *The 1 5/16 ins hub nut will probably need a socket and long extension to free it, and you may have trouble preventing the hub rotating. If putting the car into 1st gear doesn't do the trick, you will have to replace the road wheel and lower it to the ground.*

9 *The hub (with conical oil seal collar inside) should then pull clear of the half-shaft splines without too much difficulty, and usually without the need for special tools. However, if you do encounter an obstinate hub, you may have to hire an extractor if you don't already possess one (note that different extractor tools are of course required for wire and standard wheel cars).*

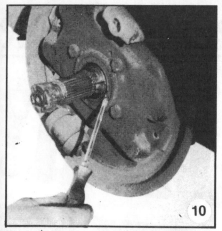

The hub oil seal is then revealed, and if that's been leaking it will have to be removed.

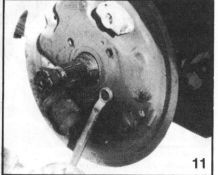

The backplate has to come off for this operation, by undoing four nuts.

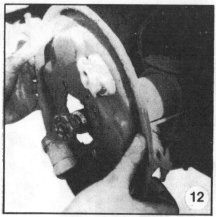

After disconnecting the brake pipe, and the handbrake (remove the clevis pin which secures the cable to the lever), the backplate can be drawn clear.

The hub oil seal is inside a housing which is sandwiched between back plate and axle — if the leak is simply due to pressurisation, it may be re-usable.

Once dismantled, wash off all parts in paraffin or petrol and examine them for wear; and when in doubt — replace! It's the cheapest

If you need to remove the half-shaft and bearing, you can either use the special tool (which incorporates a slide hammer) or employ this method to withdraw it. Just replace the hub and nut, then reverse-fit the brake drum as shown and use soft-face hammer or mallet (a hard one could shatter the drum) to extract shaft. Bearing can then be pressed from shaft if required.

policy in the long run. Reassembly is the usual process of fitting the parts back in reverse order, the half-shaft needing to be driven back into position (a special tool is available for this but most people manage without). Refit your new oil seal with its lips facing into the axle. Remember to keep everything clean, especially the hydraulic brake parts. The braking system will, of course, need to be bled after this work, and the brake shoes re-adjusted.

NEXT MONTH
Stripping out the door furniture on both roadsters and GTs.

CONTINUED FROM PAGE 25

MGB Restoration!

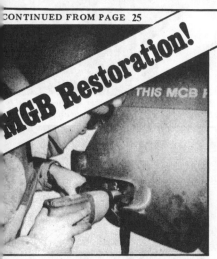

The same procedure is carried out where the panel meets the rear valance.

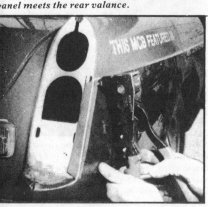

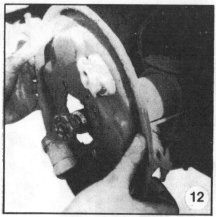

The front repair panel is similarly offered up and secured. At this stage the door must be accurately re-hung to check that the door aperture gap is correct with the new panel in place abutting the door shut pillar and sill.

The pop rivets being installed after lining up. Note too how the repair panel overlaps the rear light area.

NEXT MONTH
Tackling the rear inner wing repairs.

When adjustments to the two repair panels have been completed satisfactorily, it will become clear where to cut the overlapping and redundant piece of front panel away. This must be done accurately, with careful final trimming to achieve a good butt join, which will be gas welded.

Here, the brazed/welded joins are being linished flat ready for the minor filling which will be necessary before painting operations begin.

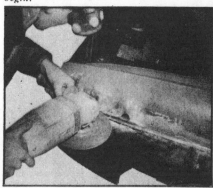

PRACTICAL CLASSICS PROJECT CAR

MGB Restoration! PART 9

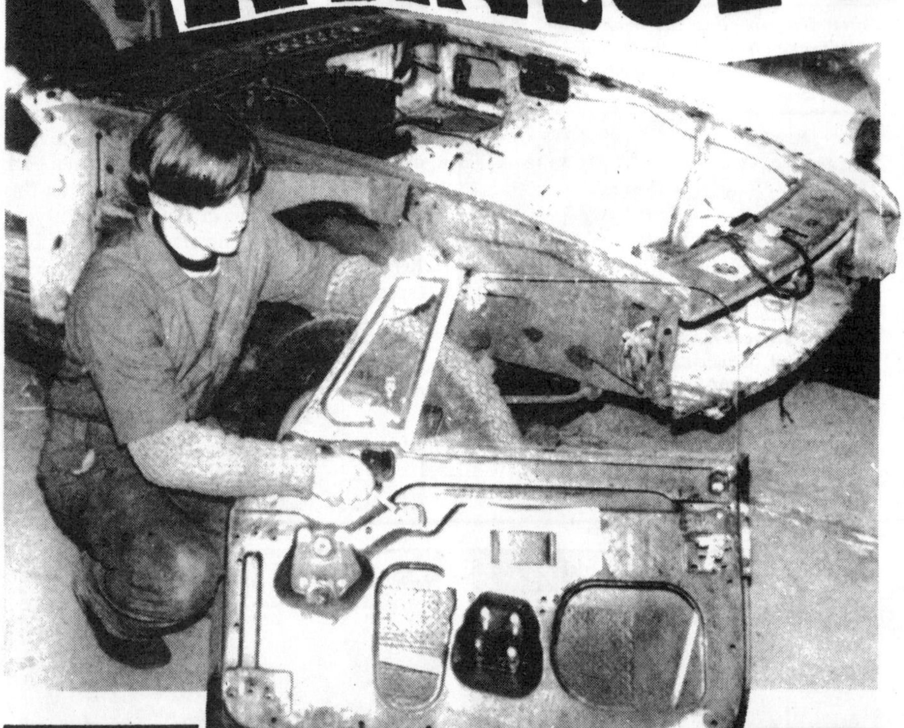

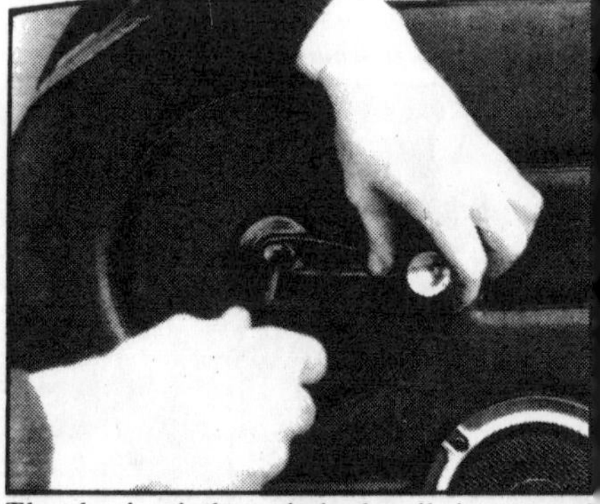

The plastic window winder handle is removed by undoing the centre Philips screw: note that these handles are very liable to breaking.

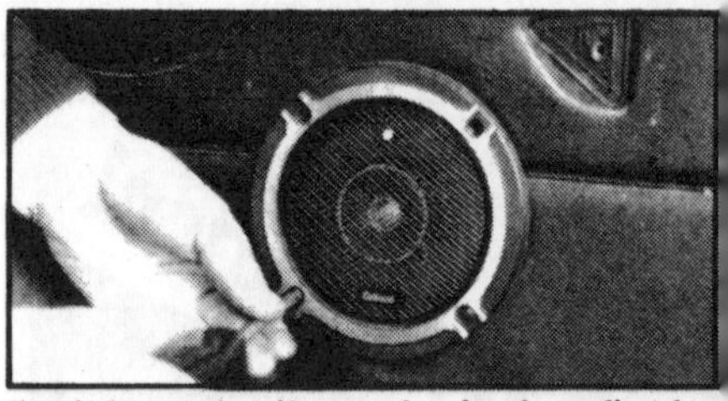

Don't forget that if a speaker has been fitted to the door casing, this must come away as well.

Removing door locks and fittings is the subject of this month's MGB feature from John Hill's MGB Centre.

Major repair work on the door shell, or swopping doors from one car to another, usually entails stripping all the parts off. Here, using a 'Mk III' door, we detail the procedure followed step-by-step, also noting some of the more common fail-points.

Early doors are different in a number of respects, and we also cover the dismantling of a 'Mk I' GT door to illustrate some of these for the benefit of those of you with the earlier model. GT doors are also a little different, but the dismantling/reassembly procedures are essentially the same.

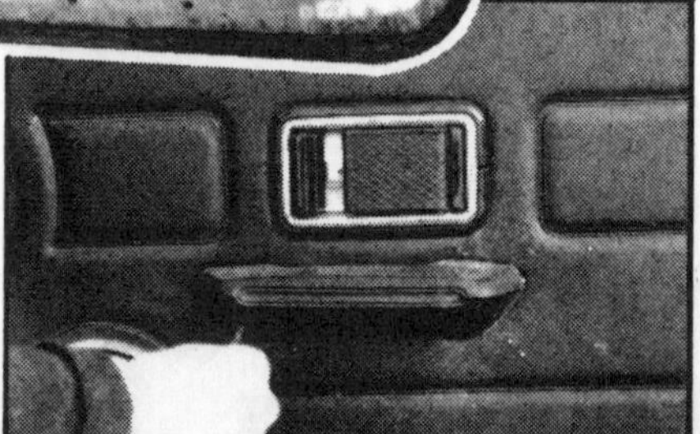

Door casing removal begins with unscrewing the two Philips headed screws securing the armrest.

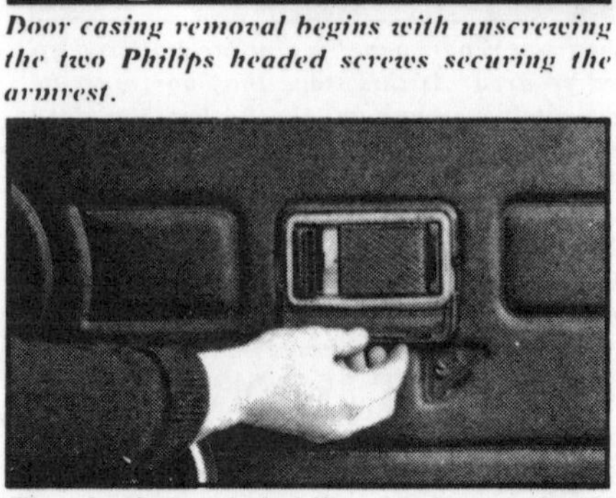

The plastic bezels holding the door casing in place around the release handle are slid out, top and bottom.

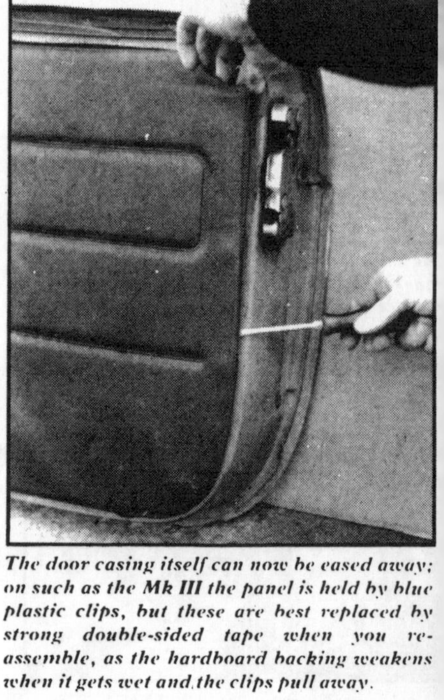

The door casing itself can now be eased away; on such as the Mk III the panel is held by blue plastic clips, but these are best replaced by strong double-sided tape when you re-assemble, as the hardboard backing weakens when it gets wet and the clips pull away.

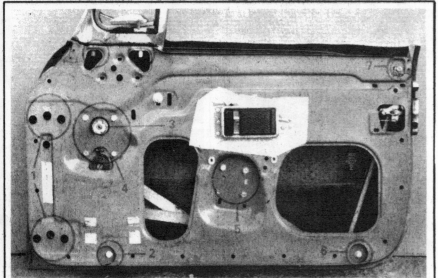

Door furniture attachment points: 1) door hinge screws; 2) ¼-light frame bottom mounting; 3) window winder handle attachment; 4) bolts securing regulator; 5) bolts securing regulator extension; 6) rear channel securing bolt (2 screws early cars); 7) rear channel top securing bolt; 8) ¼-light frame nuts.

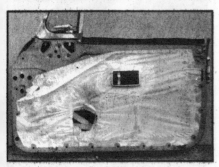

Underneath is a plastic liner intended to stop water getting to the casing; make up a new one if torn, and secure with strong tape and/or adhesive.

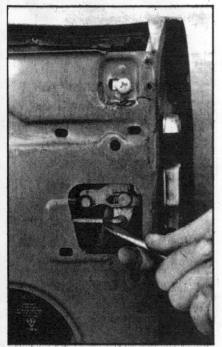

To remove the interior door lock and handle, first prise off the clip holding the latch release rod.

Do the same with the (upper) lock control rod, and pull both rods free from their bushes.

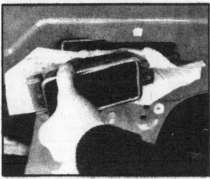

Undo the three screws holding the door lock in place and pull free complete with latch release rod.

Remove lock itself by undoing the cross-headed screws.

The channel in which the window glass slides at the rear is removed by undoing the top fixing screw . . .

. . . and the securing bolt (from captive nut) at the bottom. Earlier cars had two bolts here.

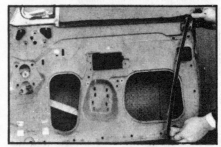

The rear channel removed; the felts can be renewed, but corrosion in the bottom bracket often causes failure, and a replacement may have to be fitted.

For releasing the glass and window regulator mechanism, the 7/16 ins AF bolts securing the regulator extension to the door must be undone.

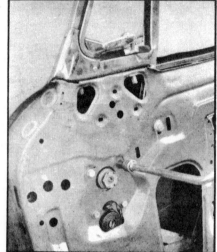

The regulator itself is released by undoing four more bolts. When removing the regulator note which of the two positions is used.

The quarter-light frame at the bottom has to be released to allow a gap for the regulator mechanism to pass through; note that the door glass can be removed at this stage (it had broken on this particular door).

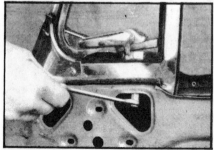

Removal of the quarter-light frame continues with the undoing of the nut underneath here . . .

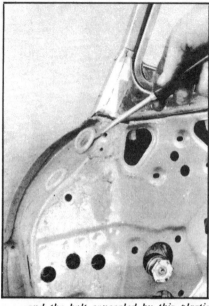

. . . and the bolt concealed by this plastic grommet.

The assembly can now be eased out of the door. The GT quarter-light differs from the roadster one in that it is taller and radiused at the top, and also allows for the different windscreen rake. Strip and rebuild procedures are identical though.

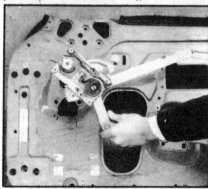

There is now room to extricate the regulator mechanism. Note that the mechanisms are handed, and differ between roadster and GT models. Typical fail points are a broken spring, stripped cogs, or seized pivot points due to corrosion.

Early doors have screw-on trim panels; note that screw holes corrode and it is usually necessary to make new holes if fitting new casing.

These doors also have padded cappings which are unscrewed from either end.

This is the 'Mk I' door release mechanism; the rear end is released by removing the circlip which connects it to the door lock.

Removing the door glass from an early GT door, having released the channeling in which it runs.

On early doors the ¼-light frame and rear channel are each held by 2 Philips-headed screws; these usually seize, however, and are best drilled out.

NEXT MONTH
Re-skinning the MGB door

MGB Restoration!

PART 10

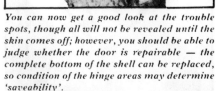

A new door for your MGB will cost around £80, but the chances are you can repair it for a fifth of this cost if you follow this simple re-skinning procedure. We report from John Hill's MG Centre.

You can now get a good look at the trouble spots, though all will not be revealed until the skin comes off; however, you should be able to judge whether the door is repairable — the complete bottom of the shell can be replaced, so condition of the hinge areas may determine 'saveability'.

Re-skin a moderately rusted MGB door and it will compare well with a brand new one. You can also apply the formula to a really badly rotten door, and although the repairs may not be so long-lasting in this case, the 20% saving in cost over a new door could still make it a worthwhile proposition — especially if the remainder of the car doesn't warrant a bigger investment.

In any case, new doors are only available for cars 1968-onwards, so if you own an older MGB, you are faced with the choice of re-skinning or changing over to the later-type door with its attendent different door locks and window regulator mounting points. With the constantly improving parts situation for MGBs this dilemma may not always be present, but it is certainly something which faces owners of earlier cars at the moment.

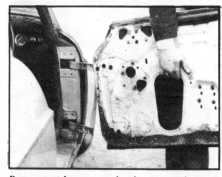

Door must be removed prior to repair; undo the large Philips screws holding door to hinge (use a wrench on the screwdriver to get the leverage, rather than employ an impact driver which can damage a weak door shell), instead of removing hinges from car — which also involves undoing a bolt hidden by the front wing. Also, the counter-sunk threaded door screws are no longer available from BL..

It's important that you don't distort the frame by hammering and levering the skin off the shell; use of a linishing disc on a sander applied to the edge of the skin will weaken the metal without distortion.
A heavy-duty angle grinder makes quick work of linishing through the skin edges, but if you haven't one (or cannot hire one) an ordinary electric drill with an abrasive disc will do the job too — it just takes longer.

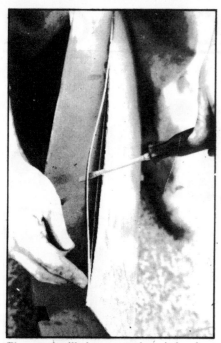

The metal will then part where it has been folded over the door frame; note that there are hardly any welds holding the skin on, merely the fold-over.

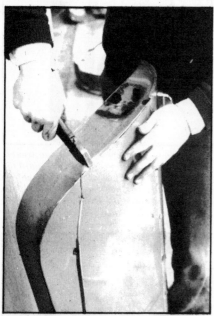

The remains of the flange can be removed with pliers, during which operation you may well find rust even in areas apparently sealed by paint.

The only time a hacksaw has to be applied is where the quarterlight frame seats; a cut is made right through the centre of the slots.

The old skin is now more or less free and can be opened out like this; all that is now holding it are a few spot welds on the leading edge, which will soon weaken with flexing, or with careful use of a hammer and chisel if necessary. We strongly advise you to wear thick protective gloves.

Only now are all the rusted areas disclosed; corners and bottom flange are usually the worst affected. Also arrowed are the hinge points — note their triangulated reinforcements and captive hinge plates; in bad cases these too can need attention.

If you've followed our advice regarding the removal of the old skin, distortion of the door frame should have been kept to a minimum. However, breaking the spot welds at the front edge of the door may necessitate a little dressing with hammer and dolly.
Go all round the door frame and ensure that none of the other flanges are distorted.

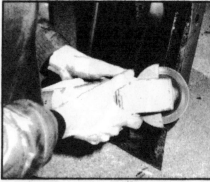

The door frame can then be cleaned up with a sanding disc, paying special attention to the leading edge where the spot welds have been broken, and to any surface rust.

This is the new door skin, a pressing so that each one is certain to fit the door shell accurately. It comes complete with all cut-outs and even ¼-light frame bolt holes. The inside of the skin can be painted with an anti-rust primer at this stage, a treatment worthwhile applying to the bare door shell too.

Lay the skin face down on a clean, flat floor and place the door frame on top of it. Any distortion of the frame will quickly show up all the way round as the two surfaces meet (or don't meet as the case may be).

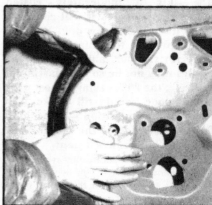

As the frame is very weak without its skin, it can easily be adjusted to ensure it fits the new skin, often simply by hand as shown here. This sort of 'tweaking' may seem brutal but is the correct procedure; above all, make the frame fit the skin, never the other way round.

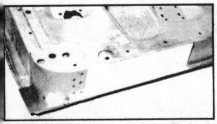

If the frame itself is rotten, you've obviously got to repair it first. Various repair sections are available, or making your own would not be too difficult if you have some experience in metalworking. The front bottom corner is usually the worst place for corrosion.

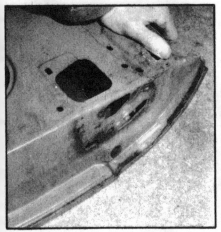

Actual skin fitting commences with laying skin on flat, firm surface such as chipboard. The idea is to fold the skin over the frame which is placed on top of the skin. Commence folding where the frame is stepped for the chrome moulding.

After tapping the skin edge up vertically, fold it over to lie flush with the frame, again starting from the moulding line. Make firm for 3-4 ins before moving to the other side of the moulding line, folding over for another 3-4 ins.

Then go to the one right-angled corner of the door, and fold skin over for approx. 4 ins in each direction.

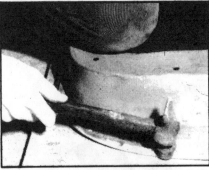

Now return to the rear edge, the door being supported and rolled on the flat surface so that the flange has a solid backing where the hammer strikes.

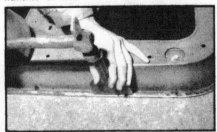

The bottom flange is difficult to hammer over due to the close proximity of the frame, so a blunted bolster chisel (of the sort used by bricklayers!) is the best tool to employ here.

Gaps may appear as the job proceeds, which means pulling the door frame back into position — not bending up more door skin. Note that the door is always held so that at each hammer stroke the point of contact is flat against the 'floor'.

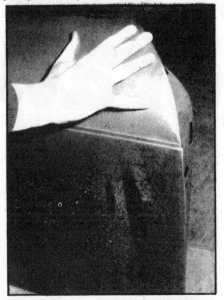

During the job, the outer skin should be inspected and felt for possible damage and rippling through 'working' of the skin during the hammering of the flange.

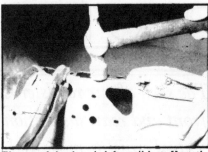

The top of the door is left until last. Here the new skin overlaps half of the old one in the ¼-light frame area, which has been left. It is dressed flat and clamped at both ends.

Only a very limited amount of welding is needed to secure the skin at this point, between the ¼-light frame holes.

The last weld — a very short run where the skin meets the frame at the top rear. The door is now ready for painting.

How you go about preparing the old door and fitting the new skin is explained by the photographs. It is one of the few large-scale body repair jobs which can be tackled by an enthusiast without any special skills, and the results are very satisfying. Very little welding/brazing is required, and if you don't have this equipment, you can simply take the door to a welder at the end stage.

NEXT MONTH
Repairs to the main bodyshell.

The shell of our roadster is stripped of front and rear suspension, and the central cross-member and jacking point repaired. More news from John Hill's MG Centre.

PART 11

MGB Restoration!

When carrying out fairly extentive repairs to the underside of the car, John Hill prefers to relieve the shell of all possible weight and turn it over, or at least onto its side, so that the job can be approached with perfect visibility and ease of access. It certainly beats scrabbling about on your back with bits and pieces dropping onto you!

The MGB is just about light enough for this to be done without too much aggravation,

although an alternative is the Carolla which we ourselves use occasionally (this device bolts to the car's hubs, and the car is rolled over using a special frame). However, if you decide to get the shell on its side (or back) without special equipment, take the greatest care because you could easily break a leg, or worse, if it drops. At your own risk!

Naturally the front suspension, which is mounted on a cross beam, and the rear axle together add up to a lot of weight, and so John Hill took these off as shown in the pictures. They do, in any case, require stripping and

rebuilding so this fits in with the restoration programme on the 'B' anyway.

The actual bodywork repairs we cover this month concern the central cross member and the jacking point at the end of it. This is a common area for rot in an MGB, and can result in the jacking point breaking free during a wheel-changing operation — not something to be enjoyed on a rainy night! The parts (cross member repair section and jacking point) are obtainable off the shelf and are not too difficult to fit, as John's sequence of photographs show. It should be said, of

To complete the stripping of the shell, the front suspension must come out. Start by undoing the front brake pipes.

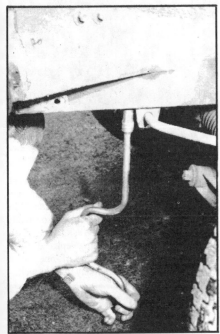

Make sure that no brake line connects front sub-frame to the bodyshell — on this car a previous owner has joined two pipes here with a union making separation easier (normally this is a straight run of pipe here).

The anti-roll bar brackets must be removed by unbolting from front chassis legs.

The steering is disconnected starting with the ball joints on the steering arms; then with the steering on full left lock (RHD cars), undo and remove the nut and pinch bolt which secures the steering col. UJ to the splines. The main ¾ ins AF nuts that hold the front sub-frame to the body can then be tackled (2 on each side), the frame supported by a jack.

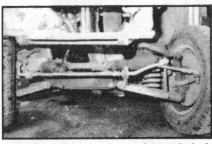

If desired (and you have an assistant) the body can be lifted off the front suspension assembly; or, before the assembly is unbolted, the car can be placed on axle stands with the wheels off the ground, and the sub-frame supported by a jack which can be lowered when the assembly is released (in which case the wheels are taken off first).

The complete front suspension unit can even be rolled about on its own wheels, to a convenient spot for cleaning and/or re-conditioning — a subject we will be covering later.

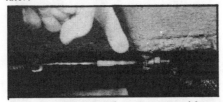

The rear axle removal commences with undoing the handbrake cable mechanism, located inside the propshaft tunnel. Undo the adjuster nut shown here on the end of the cable, and pull the cable out of the operating lever. The cable retaining clip (to left of hand) is released by undoing nut inside car, on the tunnel behind the driver's seat.

Remove the propshaft by undoing the flanges at the rear axle UJ; mark both flanges so that balance is maintained on reassembly.

This isn't actually our car, but the picture serves to show that the exhaust must be removed before the axle can be lowered.

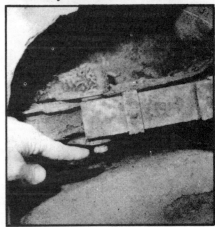

If you want to expend the minimum amount of effort, springs can be left bolted to the axle; just undo both dampers from rear chassis rail, undo front spring eye-bolts, rear shackles and flexible brake pipe. Then wheel out axle assembly from under car, after lowering it on the jack which has been supporting it during the operation (rear of car on axle stands of course).

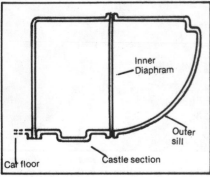

Inner Diaphram

Outer sill

Car floor

Castle section

Now back to the bodywork: to recap, the inner and outer sills, and the bottom 'castle section' or sill floor, have all been replaced in previous episodes, and are shown in cross section in this diagram.

For general ease of working, and to avoid weld dropping in your eyes, the now stripped-out shell can be turned on its side, resting on old tyres (not on wheels!) and properly supported — John Hill used two engine hoists, and a timber wedge bolted to the shell. If you do adopt this method, use extreme care, plenty of assistance, and a foolproof method of supporting the shell if left at an angle instead of being turned completely upside down (which is a further alternative).

In order to finish off the welding along back edge of new castle section, the area of bodyshell adjacent to it was cleared of old sealant by warming and wire brushing.

With the car in this position, you will find it easy to make sure that the castle section already installed meets the bodyshell correctly; where a gap exists, it can be eliminated using a hammer.

The welding of the castle section to the main floor can now be completed; the welds at the sill bottom can also be tidied now that you have easy access.

We now move on to the jacking point and central box-section cross-member; the outer few inches of this and the jacking point usually suffer from rot on an elderly 'B'. Here the end of the cross member is being cleaned-up, with the old jacking point and corroded metal already removed. New cross member end finds a temporary home on chassis rail.

The castle section had been fitted so that it ran under the cross-member end; note that all rusty metal has been cut from the cross member.

The cross member repair section, designed to fit over the original, reinforcing it and providing ample welding points for proper location. But it must never be fitted over unsound metal, which must be cut away first.

The repair section is positioned, and tacked in place. Note that the two outer corners have been folded at right angles to meet up with the castle section inner sides.

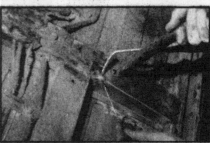

The inner end of the repair section is then held in position, and tack welded.

The side flanges of the repair section are also welded, and the jacking point offered up and welded into position too.

course, that the replacement of these items can be done without stripping the car out completely, or even turning it on its side. Note however that this particular job is normally done while the sills themselves, and the 'castle section' underneath, are being replaced too as they are all inter-related and if one bit is rotten, the other parts are likely to be as well.

NEXT MONTH
More mechanical/chassis reconditioning.

Our MGB roadster's shell is cleaned-off prior to the important step of fitting the outer panels.

MGB Restoration!

PART 12

Virtually all the repairs to the bare bodyshell are now complete, with one possible exception — John Hill reckons that the front fairing under the grille aperture looks a bit second-hand so that will probably be replaced by a new one. Meanwhile, it's been a case of thoroughly cleaning and preparing the basic shell to accept the new outer panels which it will begin to receive from next month's instalment onwards.

This is tedious work, but cleaning off the engine bay, inner wings and underside is very important if you are to end up with a car that looks good even from underneath and will resist dirt and water during future use. How far you go in the search for a good underside finish is up to you, but the essential part of the job is to remove all traces of rust, especially from corners which could collect mud in the future, and where new outer panels will mate up to. Otherwise, your efforts with the rest of the car — however good it looks from outside — will be wasted because rust and rot will

inevitably set in again once the car is back on the road.

With every movable item unscrewed and with the front wings off, our shell was at an ideal stage for a process which is really second-to-none for achieving results in the cleaning process — sand blasting. There is nothing like it for taking rust off metal, even deep pitting being stripped by the blast of particles to 'bright' metal, and it is capable of reaching

The sand-blasting of the B's shell in operation; the car was slung over the end of a flatbed truck to provide good access at an easy working height. Gear looks as if it has been borrowed from Star Wars, but is essential to protect the operator; it even has its own air supply to the helmet.

into corners and seams in a way which is virtually impossible to duplicate by hand.

MGB Restoration!

If you haven't seen it done before, sand or bead blasting is near-miraculous in the way it turns rusty metal into 'new'.

The MGB Centre has its own equipment, but there are a number of companies which specialise in coming round to your premises to do the work, or you can trailer your car to them. The cost of the operation is not great when you consider that five or seven hours work by a sand-blasting operative will probably save you many weeks with a scraper and sanding disc — and you still wouldn't achieve the same standard of finish.

There are few snags to sand-blasting, but if you want the operator to come to you, check with him first as to the conditions in which he'll be working — he may consider your front garden unsuitable for environmental reasons, as even with the use of portable screening, the dust fall-out is considerable. Some firms use a more advanced form of blasting using aluminium or other metal particles which can be even more effective than sand, with less fall-out, but still check with the operator first.

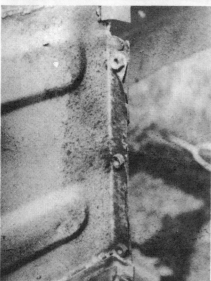

One thing the process does do is to show up any weak spots in the metal — by removing every last trace of rust, you may well discover holes and feathered edges in what appeared to be sound panels beforehand.

Front fairing will be one of the last 'inner body' panels to be replaced, and the job will be covered next month.

Then it is unwise to blast a car which is not totally stripped — the sand or other 'media' is incredibly penetrating and will invariably get into headlining, trim and even mechanical components if they have been left on the car.

The other point to watch is the weather — a damp atmosphere promotes clogging of the equipment as the water separator cannot cope with the moisture content of the air being compressed; damp sand is also fatal. Additionally, you should make arrangements to immediately protect panels which have been sand-blasted, because the totally clean, bare metal is very susceptible to rust — again, a merely damp atmosphere can turn a freshly blasted panel bright red within hours — minutes almost. The best idea is to have a prepared spraying area well away from the blasting operation and as each detachable panel is finished, take it there to spray at once with primer.

The same goes for the bare shell when that is finished, though be ready to spend some time with brush and vacuum cleaner to remove the sand or media first (ask the operative to give the car a good blow over with his compressed air equipment before he goes — that'll do the main part of the cleaning up job). An alternative to painting panels immediately is to spray them with light oil, which will afford adequate protection for some weeks, though it does mean careful cleaning off again with thinners before you do come to apply paint.

One word about the sand-blasting of outer panels — thin gauge metal can be dented or rippled by the high air pressures involved especially if it is not held rigid by being mounted on a car; so take the operator's advice before such items as outer wings and doors are tackled.

NEXT MONTH
We begin to fit the B's new outer panels.

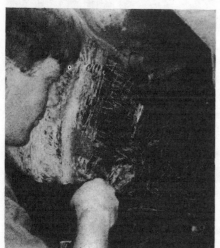

Sand-blasting is not very good at removing underbody sealants, which are resiliant and bounce the media off. These can really only be dealt with by patiently scraping off by hand. We've found that spraying with Waxoyl first softens the stuff up — paint remover is useless by the way!

42

MGB Restoration!

PART 13

This month we follow the replacement of our roadster's front tray at John Hill's MGB Centre

The MGB's front tray (or radiator duct panel as the parts book calls it) covers the forward part of the car's integral chassis and carries the oil cooler. In this position it is susceptible to rust (especially adjacent to the inner front wings) and to accident damage, and so often needs attention if not complete replacement.

Initially, John Hill considered that the rust damage on our car's tray was confined to the outer corners, and could be rectified simply by separating the tray from the inner wings and cutting out a 'triangle' of metal from the tray outboard of the two chassis legs. But as work progressed it became evident that other parts of the tray were not in too good a condition, so it was decided to go the whole hog and replace the entire panel. However, the 'outer corner' method of repair is quite acceptable if the damage is local to these parts of the tray.

Most of the work involved in the replacement of the tray centres around the releasing of the spot welds holding it in place. These can be dealt with by drilling each weld individually (not necessarily penetrating right through both pieces of metal) and then gently breaking the weakened spot weld with a screwdriver, working down the line of welds. As shown in the pictures, this work can be shortened by leaving the centre part of the tray in position over the chassis and cross member, provided it is in good condition. However, this does mean that on fixing the new tray, the spot welder has to cope with three thicknesses of metal instead of two — and it is thus especially important to see that they are all in very close contact with each other.

As we often point out, the use of a spot welder is by no means essential (although these can be hired if you want the neatness and speed which they can bring in reasonably skilled hands) and a gas torch can be used with equal effect on this job; even brazing would be permissible here as the tray is not a structural member. What is required in either case is the conscientious cleaning and dressing of flanges to ensure a good fit and strong welds — not difficult with this particular job. The operation was completed by lightly grinding back the spot- and gas-welds for appearance's sake, and priming to prevent rust forming.

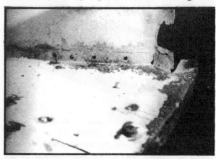

The old tray was removed beginning with the drilling out of the spot welds holding it to the front inner wing.

The tray was then cut through adjacent to the chassis member and a triangular section removed, as at first the intention was to just replace these outer corners.

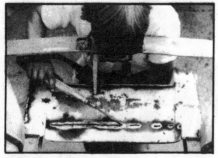

However, the tray turned out to be in rather poor condition overall, so total removal was decided on. Here Dave Cartwright proceeds to cut away the remaining sections of the tray from the chassis members.

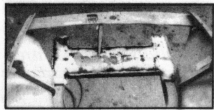

This is what the area looked like with all the outer rusted or damaged parts of the tray removed from the chassis legs and front cross-member. A welding torch was used but similar results could be obtained with a hacksaw or cutting disc.

Separating this tray from each chassis member would have meant a great deal of work breaking the many spot welds, so as this part of the tray was rust free, it was left in place and the edges cleaned back to the box member flanges.

The top of the tray was stripped of paint and linished to bright metal; where bolts or screws securing the oil cooler etc would penetrate, sections were cut from the tray to avoid fouling problems later on.

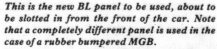

This is the new BL panel to be used, about to be slotted in from the front of the car. Note that a completely different panel is used in the case of a rubber bumpered MGB.

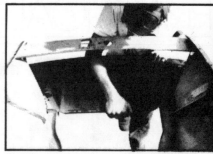

As with virtually all new panels, even original manufacturer ones, an exact fit is not obtained first time, and minor adjustments to flanges (or sometimes much more!) are usually needed before the panel can be permanently secured.

However, fitting a new tray is not complicated and soon the spot welder was brought into play for the first locating welds. Note the cross-member and chassis member flanges to which the new tray is being welded.

Spot welding is not essential and indeed the tray flange to inner wing was gas-welded into place, using a series of tacks.

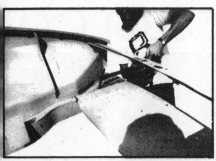

Spot-welding continued along all the lengths of chassis member flanges.

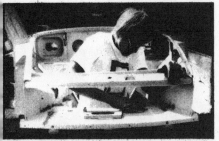

The new tray had been undercoated before installation, and to ensure a good spot weld, the paint needed to be cleaned off wherever the spot welder was to be applied.

During spot welding it is essential that the thicknesses of metal are in close contact, particularly when three are involved as here (new panel, part of the old, and the chassis member flanges). The clamping action of the spot welder itself helps but dressing (even with the wrong type of hammer!) is still required first.

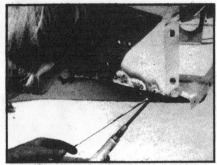

Here the rearward seam of the front cross-member is being spot welded to the new tray. Again, this operation could have been carried out using gas welding or brazing equipment instead.

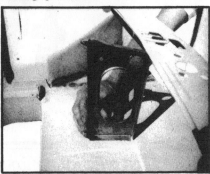

Parts of the lower edge of the inner ring were found to be pin-holed with rust, and so needed building up with weld.

This is the new reinforcement panel which supports the bonnet catch panel above.

This was carefully positioned using the old spot welds left on the top panel as a guide.

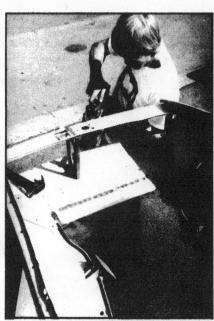

The reinforcement panel's flanges were then welded to the new tray and to the top panel.

The spot welds were tidied using an angle grinder.

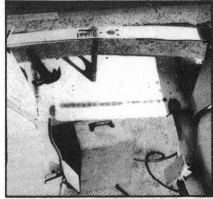

Almost there — the new tray in place with the reinforcement panel also spot welded into position. Just some more tidying of spot welds and then priming to protect any areas of bare metal are neede to complete the job.

NEXT MONTH
Front wing and door fitting —
the big struggle!

MGB Restoration!

PART 14

Fitting of the major front-end panels — wings, bonnet and doors — feature in this month's instalment from the MG Centre, Redditch.

As is always the case at this stage of a rebuild, our MGB roadster shell suddenly began to look like a car again as it collected its wings and doors — now that inner and outer sills, wheelarches and much else on the basic shell have all either been replaced or repaired. New BL front wings were employed (and MGB owners are indeed fortunate that you can still get these, even if, at £95, they are not exactly cheap), our previously re-skinned doors, and — perhaps a trifle extravagantly — a brand new bonnet.

Would-be restorers often fall into the trap of expecting that brand-new factory panels will fit straight on a car with virtually no hassle, especially if the new component is bolt-on like the MG's front wings. However, often nothing is farther from the truth and what appears to be half an afternoon's work frequently develops into a struggle lasting several long weekends; or, at least, it does if you want to end up with doors which don't foul and gaps which are nicely even all round. And having forked out for new wings it's rather a waste of money if you don't get it all right.

There is no doubt about it, outer panel fitting is a skilled job. Almost anyone can,

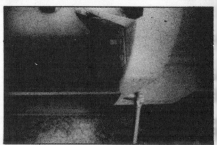

Hinges had been removed from car for cleaning and to allow tidying and inner protection of the door pillars; they are handed so RH musn't be confused with LH. Later MGBs than ours have modified hinges to allow the doors to stay open.

pictures, and they should enable you to achieve a very tolerable result on your own car —provided that the shell has, of course, been repaired accurately beforehand in the places where it counts (replacement sills properly aligned etc). But if you haven't tackled such jobs before, just allow yourself plenty of time and be determined to work to the highest standards you can manage — as we said, we are now beginning on the parts which really show when you eventually drive your 'B' round to see your friends or to a club meeting!

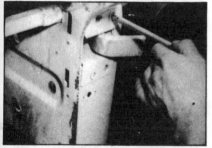

Top hinge bolt being tightened; door is offered up to body using rear wing and sill as datum points.

given time, adequately patch up the internals of a rusted car, where the appearance of the finished job isn't critical and where dimensions aren't crucial; but when it comes to the outside of the car — which everyone sees — it's a different story. You *have* to get it right then, and this requires time, patience and experience if you are to finish up with a really good job (and thus a really good car). No amount of shiny paint afterwards is going to disguise doors which foul or wing/bonnet lines which start off one end 3/8-ins wide and run out to ½-ins at the other . . . .

The fitting techniques as applied to MGB doors and wings are shown by John Hill in the

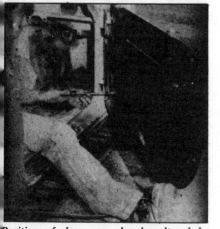

Hinges are also secured by Phillips screws; just two are being replaced (diagonally) in each plate so that latter can be moved to adjust the door fit.

Position of door can also be altered by loosening the hinge attachments inside the door shell itself — note method of adjusting door upwards with third 'hand'!

After each alteration the door must be closed and checked at all points to ensure that gaps are equal all round, there is no fouling, and that top lines up with top of body.

A small amount of dressing of the door flange is permissable during later stages when further movement of the door on its hinges doesn't do the trick. Besides the gaps all round the door, moulding on door shoulder must line up with similar line on rear wing.

The door is now almost a satisfactory fit, though allowance must be made for the weight of the door furniture (glass, lock and winding mechanisms and trim all add up to many pounds in weight), and the affect of rubber seals — which means that final adjustment may be needed when all these are in place.

Before front wing replacement is attempted, the area it will cover must be protected so that the next rebuild will be 20 years away.

The door hinge pillar area seen being painted in the previous picture is closed off by a removable mud shield with rubber flap seal attached; this bolts on at the rear of the front wheel arch, where mastic is applied to ensure a waterproof seal.

This closing panel should come painted from the manufacturer — if it hasn't, don't forget to do it yourself before bolting it in place.

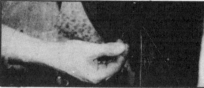

Note that the closing panel is held on by only four bolts, so ensure that their captive nuts are in good condition — particularly as this panel may have to come off again in the future for further adjustment of doors or for radio aerial installation.

First job before offering up front wing to body is to apply mastic to the panels on which the wing will mount.

Examine the replacement wing carefully all over in a good light, and before fitting, carefully beat out any of the minor dents which even brand new factory wings often seem to collect.

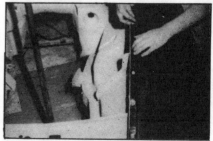

Wing is placed on the car for the first trial fit, and the securing bolts which run along the side of the engine bay are inserted.

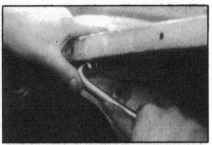

Some front wing bolts hide up behind the dash, but on a fully stripped-down car like ours access is not too difficult.

Wing bolts are not tightened fully down at this stage, to allow adjustment of the wing so that it lines up with door edge — which can be done with carefully levering.

The shape of the front wing makes it very tricky to get right first time — it's very flexible when off the car but once bolted up it is surprising how rigid and un-cooperative the assembly becomes. Here during the fitting procedure the bottom of the wing is held in the desired place by a special technique(!) while a piece of cardboard is used to check the gap between wing and door.

Wing being checked where it fits round closing panel in front wheel arch.

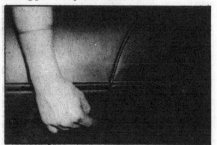

A typical problem encountered during fitting is front edge of door catching the wing as it opens; you may even have to move the door again to alleviate this fault.

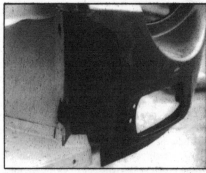

When the front wing came to be filled at the front of the car, it was found that some metal at the bottom of the inner wing where the lower bolt goes through was missing.

Accordingly a piece of metal was cut to shape, folded, clamped in place, and then welded.

The two verticle 7/16th ins bolts could then be inserted, and, with this joint also sealed with mastic, tightened up.

Bonnet hinges and bonnet are trial fitted next, with other front wing just laid in place, to check on bonnet-to-wing gaps.

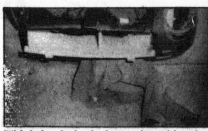

With bolts slack, the bonnet is positioned as well as possible; then to avoid raising the bonnet and risking disturbing the dimension, a fitter crawled into the engine bay and tightened the bolts up from underneath — another advantage of working on a stripped, engine-less car!

Running a hand over the three panels (scuttle, wing and bonnet) will quickly reveal if they are all level.

Meanwhile the other front wing is being lined up in conjunction with the other door and the bonnet. Held by just two or three bolts, it can be tapped back using large piece of non-damaging timber.

Still more adjustment of the bonnet was needed, careful levering being required to equalise the gaps between wings and bonnet.

Dressing the flanges is one of the final 'tidying-up' operations — they often suffer a bit during wing fitting as force sometimes has to be used to get some of the wing bolts in place. Last bolt-on body panel (yet to be fitted) goes under the radiator air intake aperture.

NEXT MONTH
Rear wing and other important body panel replacement.

MGB Restor -ation!

PART 15

When fitting a new bootlid, first thing to do is drop the lid into the aperture prior to fitting the hinges just to check that the lid itself is undistorted, and that the aperture is near enough correct.

A rather more brief episode this month, dealing with fitting a new bootlid — a simple job yet one which is not necessarily without the need for some work to get it looking right. Our major rear end repair has had to be postponed however, because of a shortage of rear wings for our roadster.

John Hill decided that it would be best to equip our car with brand-new rear wings because it is the ultimate solution to rot in that area, even though you can mostly get away with repair sections as rust doesn't often extend above the side moulding on the wing. However, on occasions it can infiltrate higher, and then there is always the case of accident damage which can't be cured except by fitting a complete new wing. So all in all, it was a job which shouldn't have been missed.

The problem is that a new wing is not immediately obtainable, so, after a remarkable

Rear end work proceeds but we're held up for a wing. Paul Skilleter reports from the MGB Centre, Redditch.

Having reassured yourself that the lid is basically correct, you can then attach it to the car via the three 7/16 ins AF bolts on each hinge.

The normal panel beating hammer was used to relieve the dents, and the fitter used his hand to feel the surface of the metal as the last few imperfections were dressed flat.

A hand is the best tool for discovering discrepancies in height between lid and body, and the entire circumference should be checked in this manner.

The final result, with a perfectly fitting bootlid — and now is the time to ensure this state of affairs, not after the car's been painted! Note also the repaired bottom half of the offside rear wing, covered in previous instalments.

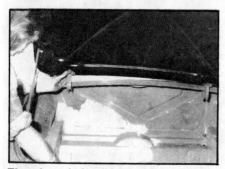

The telescopic bootlid stay is also fitted as soon as possible for convenience of working.

It is necessary to have the boot in its closed position for the final stages of dressing the boot aperture surround, so that you can be sure that a perfectly smooth line is obtained.

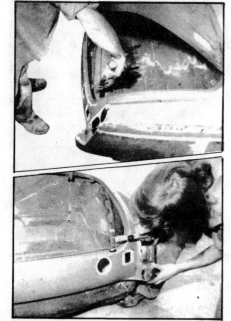

On our car, previous accident damage to the offside rear corner of the valance was discovered, and this required a certain amount of patient dressing to make good.

run of 15 episodes with the MGB Centre we may be bringing you the rear wing episode from a different source next month. The rear wing fitting will just about conclude repairs to the shell, and we shall then be going into the suspension, steering and brakes. Each of which will be stripped and completely rebuilt, to show the parts and techniques used.

This is how far we've got up until now — the nearside rear wing removed completely and the shell ready for the new wing when it materialises.

PART 16 · MGB Restoration!

Fitting a new rear wing to our roadster, the last major job to the body shell.

This shows the repair panel we saw being fitted in previous episodes, involving cutting away the original rear wing at chrome strip level. But this involves considerable linishing and filling to disguise the join, and fitting the complete outer rear wing repair panel as shown alongside makes for a better job.

This month's episode centres around a new panel which has been made available, the product of much investment in tooling by John Hill's MG Centre at Redditch. It is the complete outer section of the rear wing, up to the top beading (which comes attached to the new panel), making it ideal for anyone wishing (or needing) to go one better than a 'waist-high' repair panel, but not wishing to afford a complete new rear wing. At £28.00 plus VAT, this new panel is something like £50 cheaper than a manufacturer's rear wing complete.

In fact the fitting of this new panel to our roadster was something in the nature of a pilot exercise, using the first pressing off the line. However, fitting is a relatively straight forward job, provided you avoid damaging the original flanges and mating surfaces on the body shell when you remove the old wing.

Also take care not to cut away **too much** metal (better to leave too much on and have to trim back after offering up the new part), or to damage the shell. The big advantage of using the original flanges, especially along the top line of the wing, is that distortion caused by having to weld along the middle of the rather flexible rear wing is eliminated. Altogether a more 'classy' job.

The replacement panel too is nicely rigid, and is quite straightforward to offer up and fit to the body shell. Time should be taken at this stage to ensure that all flanges are straight, and clamp the wing in place, **before** welding, while you ensure that you have obtained a good fit. After welding, some dressing may be required adjacent to the sill, but otherwise, very little 'finishing' work is required once the panel is in place.

As is evident, this episode comes to you from John Hill's establishment, thanks to his new wing pressing, which made it possible to complete the job in time for this issue.

First the original outer wing must be removed, cutting with hacksaw up the seams and up the centre line of the rear light mounting plate. If anything, keep the cut on the outside so avoiding the removal of too much metal.

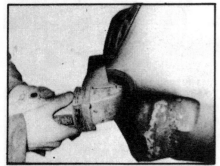

Corners are released by linishing through the metal with angle grinder (or you could use a normal electric drill).

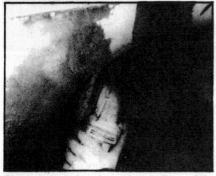

The same technique is employed all round the wheel arch; in our case the perimeter here was very strong because we had replaced inner wings and fitted that outer repair panel — normally rust will make this part of the job much easier. Inner wheel arches usually require replacing at this stage.

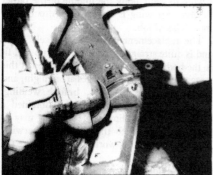

The edge of the old wing where it meets the 'B' post is linished to weaken it before carefully chiselling away.

To remove the top part of the wing, the old panel is sawn through adjacent to the metal beading, which for the moment is left in place as it is best removed with the old wing out of the way.

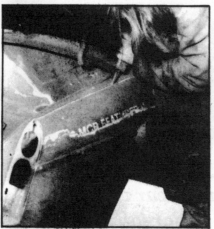

When the hacksaw can no longer be used, a pad-saw or (if you have one) an electric jigsaw continues the cut alongside the beading.

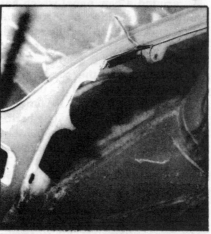

The beading can then be removed by careful use of the angle grinder and/or chisel; it will be found that the bodywork remaining on the car stays quite rigid for this operation, which is a help.

View looking up into the rear wing with the new outer panel (right) in place and clamped firmly to the body shell at frequent intervals. The fit of the new panel at door aperture is important and must be checked before any welding is done.

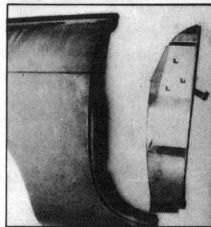

As the existing 'B' post had suffered corrosion at the bottom, it was decided to replace it with a new one which is relatively inexpensive. Here it is shown next to the rear wing panel which abuts it.

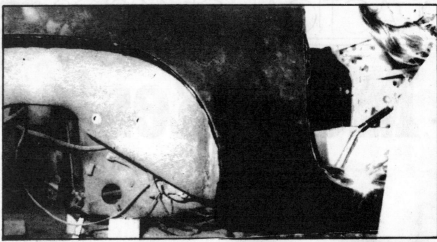

The 'B' post skin is removed by drilling out the spot welds, offering up and then clamping in position the new one, as shown here.

The rear wing panel is also welded to the sill (door step) along the top join; it has already been spot-welded along the flange at the bottom.

The rear wing is here being continuously brazed to the 'B' post after spot welding.

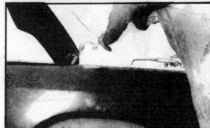

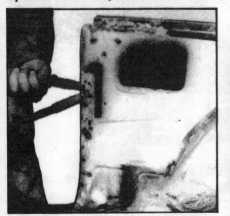

The length of the top seam of the wing was brazed after spot welding too; this increases the strength of the join while the lower temperature of the braze does not produce distortion.

The flanges will need to be dressed and the drilled-out spot welds tidied to obtain a good fit, after which the panel can be clamped and welded in position.

The outer edge of the new 'B' post being dressed prior to welding it to the new outer rear wing.

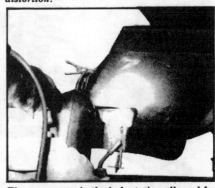

The rear seam, in the indentation allowed for the bumper, is also welded.

Here an MIG welder is being used to spot weld the new outer panel to the inner wing; conventional welding equipment could be used too, however.

NEXT MONTH
We move on from the body shell to the mechanical aspects of MGB restoration.

MGB Restoration!

PART 17

Paul Skilleter reports from the MGB Centre, Redditch, as our roadster is given its new suspension parts.

With the body shell substantially completed now, the next job was to replace the suspension, which has been stripped and rebuilt as necessary. New swivel pin kits were used, and new road springs and dampers front and rear. You can fit all these yourself, though to install new swivel pins you will need to hire a double reamer (there are two sizes of bushes in the stub-axle), or ask a garage to do that part of the job for you.

If you are completely dismantling the suspension, don't cut corners but fit all new bushes — it will be well worth it in terms of good handling, and the avoidance of trouble later. Inner wishbone bushes can be drifted out, and the technique for fitting the replacements is shown in the pictures. Examine all components (especially the lower wishbone arms and the pivot bolts) for wear and replace as necessary.

One point that must be watched during the refitting of the stub-axle is that up-and-down movement of the axle must not exceed .002 inch (.05mm) — check with a feeler gauge on

Our MG roadster, with front suspension cross-beam and all the components that will be assembled on it — wishbone arms and spring pans, stub axles, trunnion kits, bushes, dampers, brake discs and back plates, steering rack and arms, and the slightly stiffer (¾ ins diam.) anti-roll bar which we are having.

the bottom trunnion, and adjust by changing the thrust washers (which are available in various sizes). At the same time, the swivel pin must rotate freely in the trunnion.

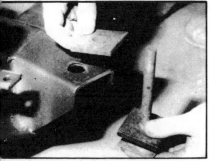

If you are undertaking a complete strip down and have dropped the sub-frame, the dampers are most easily replaced by bolting them to the frame first.

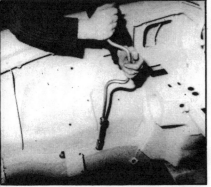

These are the sub-frame mountings; rubbers often perish and should be replaced as a matter of course if frame is removed for any reason.

The frame is jacked up to body, and the mounting bolts tightened.

Bump stop assembly can then be mounted on cross-member.

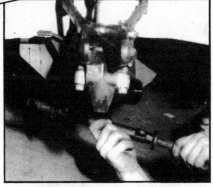

This is followed by the wishbone pivot.

The wishbone arms obviously needed new bushes; watch for elongation of the hole at the outer end, incidentally, caused by the trunnion bolt turning.

Bush is pressed into position using a suitable bolt and wide steel washers.

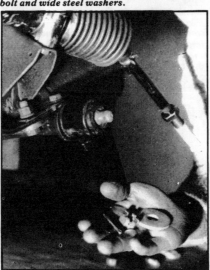

Front wishbone arm has been positioned on the pivot, where it will be secured by split-pinned nut and large washer. Ensure that arm is positioned so that with car stationary, bush is not stressed.

Spring pan then rear wishbone arm are assembled on the suspension, and anti-roll bar link installed on front arm.

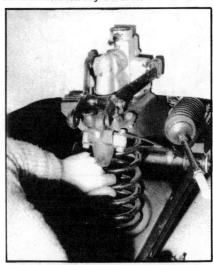

Road spring is placed in position, ready for the rebuilt stub axle to be installed as the spring is compressed by lifting the lower wishbone on the jack.

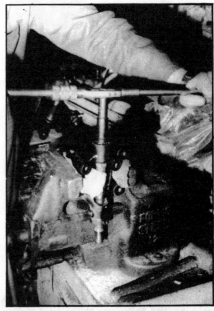

Wear of the swivel pins is common, and the solution is to replace them with new ones; this involves fitting new bushes to the stub-axle of course. This is the necessary reaming process being carried out, cutting the inserted bushes to fit the new pins.

An exploded view taken from the MGB Centre's catalogue, showing the stub-axle and its components. Swivel pin kits come with the bushes shown in fig. 3.

This exploded view shows all the components on the front cross-member.

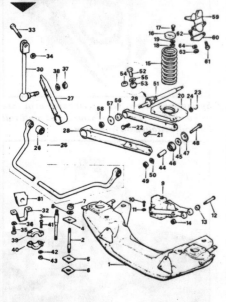

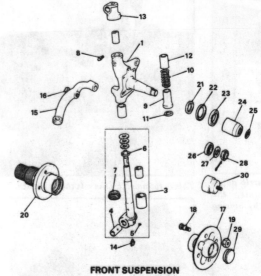

FRONT SUSPENSION

	Qty			Qty
1 Crossmember-front-RHD	1	12 Pin-fulcrum-link to shock	
2 Bolt-mounting	2	absorber arm	2
3 Bolt-mounting	2	13 Bearing-Fulcrum pin	4
4 Pad-mounting-upper	6	14 Nut	2
5 Pad-mounting-lower	2	15 Spring coil	2
6 Plate-clamp	4	16 Spigot-spring	2
7 Nut	8	17 Screw	4
8 Washer-plain	4	18 Nut	4
9 Absorber-shock	2	19 Washer-spring	4
10 Bolt	8	20 Seat-spring	2
11 Washer-spring	8	21 Screw	2

22 Screw	4
23 Nut	6
24 Washer-spring	6
25 BAR ASSEMBLY-ANTI ROLL	1
26 Bush	1
27 Arm-wishbone-front-RH	1
28 Arm-wishbone-front-LH	1
29 Arm-wishbone-rear	2
30 Loink-anti-roll bar-RH	1
Link-anti-roll bar-LH	1
31 Bearing-anti-roll bar to link	2
32 Strap-bearing	2
33 Bolt-anti-roll bar to link	2
34 Washer-spring	4
35 Screw	4
36 Washer-spring	2
37 Nut	2
38 Washer-spring	2
39 Locator-upper	2
40 Locator-lower	2
41 Screw	4
42 Washer-spring	4
44 Tube-distance link	4
45 Washer-thrust-link	4
46 Seal-link	4
47 Support	2
48 Bolt-wishbone to link	2
49 Nut	2
50 Washer-spring	2
51 Pivot-wishbone	2
52 Bolt-pivot to member	8
53 Nut-bolt-outer	4
54 Nut-bolt-inner	4
55 Washer-spring	8
56 Bush-wishbone arm	8
57 Washer-retaining	4
58 Nut	4
59 Buffer-rebound	2
60 Piece distance	2
61 Bolt	4
62 Screw	4
63 Nut	8
64 Washer-spring	8

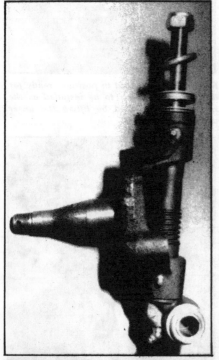

This is the assembled unit, complete with new swivel pin, ready for installation on the 'B'. Note sprung dirt shield which must be cleaned and fitted back when the swivel pin is inserted.

Here the stub-axle has been fitted to the lower wishbone, and bolted and split-pinned at the bottom. It is then swung upwards so that the top trunnion slips between the upper wishbones which have been held slightly apart by a screw-driver, as the jack raises the spring pan.

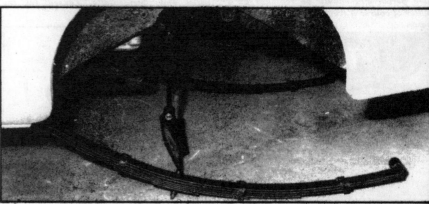

▶ *Reassembly of the rear end is somewhat more simple; front of leaf springs are bolted into place first.*

The top trunnion has now been pinned to the upper wishbone arms; steering has also been connected.

CONTINUED ON PAGE 60

MGB Restoration

PART 18

Our MGB roadster gets its engine and gearbox back — more news from the MGB Centre, Redditch.

With the bodyshell finished, it was decided to paint in the 'finish' colour all the shell except the major outer panels. There were two reasons for this — firstly, parts like the engine bay would be impossible to paint with the components in place, and secondly, the power-train and screen could be fitted and the car made road-legal for road-testing and 'sorting' before applying the final, over-all colour coat, which otherwise could easily get damaged. Thus the top of the scuttle where the screen goes was amongst the parts sprayed at this stage.

Fortunately for our budget, John Hill had determined that the engine and transmission were 'good' before the car was stripped down, and little more than routine servicing (plugs, points, oil filter etc) was required, though the rear main bearing oil seal was changed as a precaution. However, as many owners would probably like to know what's involved in completely stripping and rebuilding a B-series

engine and box, we hope to show a complete overhaul being done at the MG Centre at the end of the series, when our car is finally back on the road.

At this point, John thought it would be a good idea to go over the various MGB engine permutations. The first range of engines fitted to the MGB originally had three main bearings, and were known as the 18G (later 18GA) type. The three main bearing engine can easily be identified externally, says John, by the camshaft driven tachometer take-off at the end of the block, concealed just behind the exhaust manifold. It is worth noting though, John pointed out, that the engine back-plate/ flywheel together with the oil-seal arrangement for the three-bearing engine differ considerably from the particular engine used in our car.

With the introduction of the five main bearing engine, known as the 18GB, an oil cooler was fitted as standard and an electronic rev. counter replaced the mechanical type. Modifications to the gearbox at this time included a larger first-motion shaft, which meant that the spigot bush in the ends of the crankshaft was also increased accordingly. It is

for these very reasons that swopping engines from MGB to MGB requires caution, John warns.

The next engine changes were designated 18GD and later 18GG (ignoring for the

Prior to the engine installation, engine bay, boot, door shuts, wheelarches and interior were sprayed in the finish colour.

Next came the new clutch assembly — and a old first motion shaft from a scrap gearbox makes a very cheap clutch aligning tool.

Here is the tool in operation; about the only point to watch when offering up the clutch assembly is to ensure that the centre plate is the right way round, though re-assembly is in fact almost impossible if this mistake has been made.

Engine fitting in the 'B' is very straight-forward, though as always, make sure that your hoisting equipment is up to the job and take care, for both the car's and your own sake; engines are very heavy... Various engine mountings were used on the MGB, and the exploded diagram illustrates the types used. Note that the later series of engines up to a certain point had what is termed the 'GT' cross member mounting arrangement. There is no engine steady bracket fitted to this particular series of engines.

Later 18V engines did, however, have a revised gearbox cross-member steady bracket

A quite simple portable paint spraying plant was used and the job was done outdoors using normal air-drying cellulose; later, the final exterior coats will be applied indoors if only because of the climate!

The 18G engine as it originally came from our 'B', prior to being cleaned, serviced and painted. Road-testing prior to the car being taken off the road had shown it to be in good health.

Here the flywheel has been replaced; at the same time a new spigot bush was used because the old one was found to be spinning in the end of the crank. The bush was soaked overnight in oil — perhaps not necessary but a dry bearing here could cause an annoying squeak every time the clutch is dis-engaged.

As a precaution the rear oil seal was replaced. For this job the flywheel needs to come off, which often means struggling with the six securing bolts which are awkward to remove because of their very slim heads. This shows the new bolts used together with the special, circular lock washer which secures them. Note that the new oil seal must be replaced in the direction marked on the seal.

purposes of this article the overseas prefixes). The production run of these engines included a change point concerning components in the cylinder head and alterations to the carbs and inlet manifolding. A modified engine back-plate is also fitted to these engines, together with a pre-engaged starter which replaced the old bendix type. This contributed to the fitting of a different flywheel. Various arrangements of oil filters were fitted throughout MGB production, although it is always possible to fit the later type to any earlier engine, says John, who for this reason is installing the later cannister-type replacement oil filter on our car.

Finally, the last engine change for the UK specification MGBs was the 18V series of power units. Basically, the alterations related to slightly larger exhaust valves and revised rocker shaft pedestal drillings.

With the 'tool' still in place, the six clutch cover bolts are torqued up evenly to 25-30 lb ft.

Just before the gearbox was replaced, uneven carbon thrust bearing wear was noticed, indicating that something was amiss with this assembly. Normally the wear marks are even, but here the pattern is not concentric.

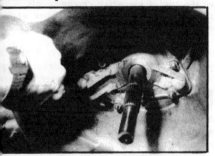

The cause of the problem was found to be in the elongated clutch pivot fork housing. Replacing the casting with a second-hand one in good condition rectified the situation.

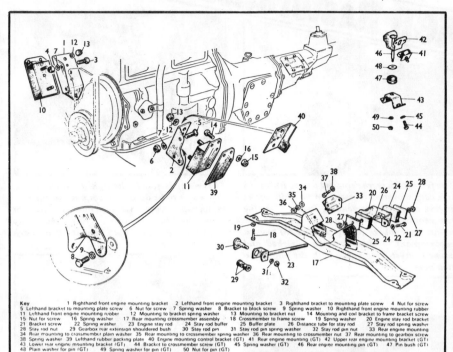

Key 1 Righthand front engine mounting bracket   2 Lefthand front engine mounting bracket   3 Righthand bracket to mounting plate screw   4 Nut for screw
5 Lefthand bracket to mounting plate screw   6 Nut for screw   7 Spring washer   8 Bracket to block screw   9 Spring washer   10 Righthand front engine mounting rubber
11 Lefthand front engine mounting rubber   12 Mounting to bracket spring washer   13 Mounting to bracket nut   14 Mounting and coil bracket to frame bracket screw
15 Nut for screw   16 Spring washer   17 Rear mounting crossmember assembly   18 Crossmember to frame screw   19 Spring washer   20 Engine stay rod bracket
21 Bracket screw   22 Spring washer   23 Engine stay rod   24 Stay rod pin   25 Buffer plate   26 Distance tube for stay rod   27 Stay rod spring washer
28 Stay rod nut   29 Gearbox rear extension shouldered bush   30 Stay rod pin   31 Stay rod pin spring washer   32 Stay rod pin nut   33 Rear engine mounting
34 Rear mounting to crossmember plain washer   35 Rear mounting to crossmember spring washer   36 Rear mounting to crossmember nut   37 Rear mounting to gearbox screw
38 Spring washer   39 Lefthand rubber packing plate   40 Engine mounting control bracket (GT)   41 Rear engine mounting (GT)   42 Upper rear engine mounting bracket (GT)
43 Lower rear engine mounting bracket (GT)   44 Bracket to crossmember screw (GT)   45 Spring washer (GT)   46 Rear engine mounting pin (GT)   47 Pin bush (GT)
48 Plain washer for pin (GT)   49 Spring washer for pin (GT)   50 Nut for pin (GT)

This diagram shows the various types of engine mountings used on the MGB. All new mountings were fitted to our car since these components are almost always found to be in poor condition due to oil leaks.

This is the all-synchromesh gearbox fitted to our car, used on 18GD engines onwards. It is easily distinguished by the fact that the starter

motor housing does not have a hole through its rear, as would be the case in earlier gearboxes to clear the starter bendix.

Prior to the engine going in, it is most important to refit the hydraulic pipe as it is very tricky to get to this at the flexible end once the engine is in position.

Assembling engine and box out of the car is much easier than fitting a gearbox to an engine already in the chassis, as one then has to align them in the confines of the bodyshell. And while they were still accessible, the units were cleaned off and painted — something else which is much easier out of the car!

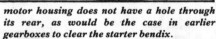

The rear mounting assembled on the crossmember, which was then fitted to the bodyshell.

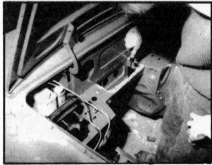

Likewise, the heater assembly is best fitted with the engine out; the unit will bed on the mastic which has been applied to this point on the bulkhead.

The fan blades were removed before fitting, as it is very tempting to use them for shifting the engine and thereby bending them. Also, the fan required painting (yellow) and the fan mounting rubbers (being pointed to) needed replacement — these become perished and cause a mystifying rattle with the engine on tick-over.

The engine is now in the right position and all that needs to be done is to connect up the new mountings. Note that the bonnet does not have to be removed, just the stay disconnected and the bonnet tied back vertically.

This is the over-run bracket referred to in the text, and seen in the exploded-view diagram of the engine mounting arrangements — it prevents the engine moving forward under heavy braking.

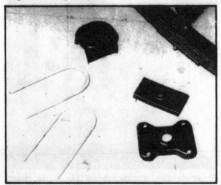

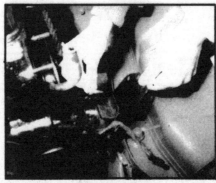

Actually inserting the engine/gearbox into an MGB is very easy, if you combine lowering the engine in at the right angle with rolling the car forward.

The mountings being bolted up — don't forget the packing plate before inserting the bolts.

again, and it is quite permissible to fit this if you are concerned about the engine riding forward on heavy braking. However, bracket no. 40 in the diagram referred to as a control bracket does a similar job to the steady bracket. In other words, says John, it prevents the engine going too far forward on its flexible mountings.

NEXT MONTH
Painting and re-fitting the bodyshell.

CONTINUED FROM PAGE 56

View showing the components of the rear suspension layout. ▶

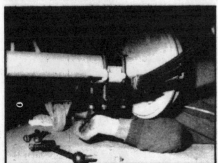

New bumper rubbers (top of picture) and 'U' bolts are recommended.

Axle is jacked into position and the spring locating plates and 'U' bolts are installed. Axle has been overhauled and painted previously, and brakes fitted — but we will be returning to this subject in the future.

REAR SPRING COMPONENTS

		Qty
1	SPRING ASSEMBLY-TOURER	2
1	SPRING ASSEMBLY REAR-GT GT	2
2	Bush	2
12	Shackle-plate (with pins)	2
13	Shackle-plate	2
14	Bush-shackle plate (Rubber)	8
15	Nut	4
16	Washer-spring	4
17	'U' bolt GT	4
17	'U' bolt-Tourer	4
18	Nut	8
19	Pedestal-bump rubber	2
20	Plate-spring locating	2
21	Pad-spring seating	4
22	Bracket-shock absorber-RH	1
	Bracket-shock absorber-LH	1
23	Pin-shackle-front end	2
24	Nut	2
25	Washer-spring	2
26	Strap-rebound	2
27	Tube-distance-strap	2
28	Nut	2
29	Washer-plain	2
30	Washer-spring	2
41	Bolt	2
32	Nut	2
33	Washer-spring	2
34	Bump rubber	2

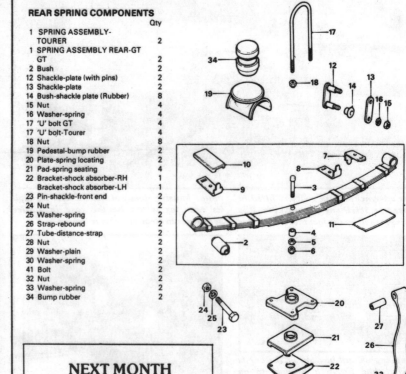

NEXT MONTH
We fit the engine and gearbox

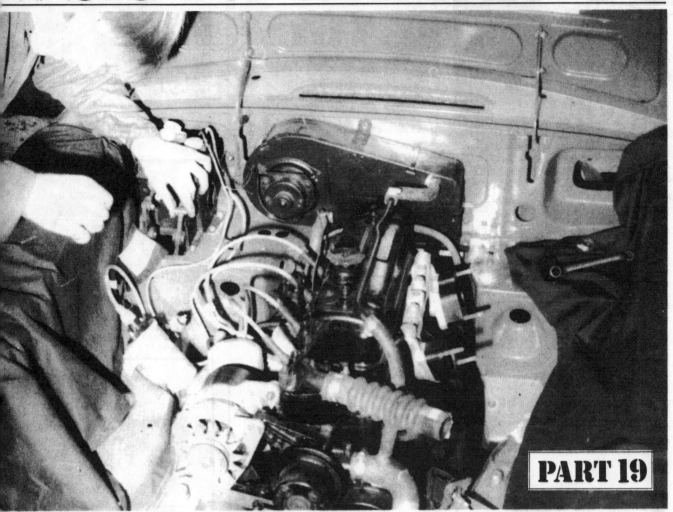

PART 19

MGB Restoration!

Engine ancilliaries and prop-shaft go back as the time draws near when the engine can be started for the first time. Paul Skilleter reports from John Hill's MGB Centre, Redditch.

This month we cover replacing the radiator, exhaust manifold, carbs and propellor shaft, all of which were examined on removal and replaced or overhauled as necessary — and when restoring an older car, it's often a shock to find how badly worn or sub-standard parts are when you take them off and give them a close look, even though they have (apparently) been performing alright when the car was being used. As they invariably play up if you put them back on in the same state, the only wise course of action is to renew or replace them now , though this is an extremely common reason why a rebuild or an overhaul turns out to be monstrously more expensive or time-consuming than the hapless owner expected when he first started the job! But nevertheless, the time and expense invested at this stage will save even more of the same later, because at least everything's already apart.

This has naturally been the MGB Centre's (and our) policy with our roadster, especially after so much work has gone into the full restoration of the body shell. Fortunately MGB mechanics are relatively simple, and replacement parts rarely present a problem, so provided you have the time, only your wallet is likely to be affected if you are a reasonably competent home mechanic. The pictures tell the story of progress since last month, and although there is still a fair way to go, it seems certain that this MGB will be joining our staff fleet in the not too distant future.

Before replacing the petrol tank, it pays to renew the simple twist-lock ring and washer which invariably leaks, and if possible the sender gauge too as it usually breaks an internal wire. Make sure lock ring is fully tightened on replacement.

A non-original replacement fuel tank was used because of the price advantage; here extra protection in the form of undersealant had been brushed on, and packing piece round filler pipe fitted (further packing strips are also used).

Captive-nut clips are cheap so fit new ones, tapping them on tank flange adjacent to the five mounting holes.

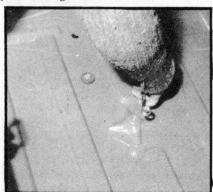

Tank has been offered up under boot floor, and the studs which also secure it are bolted up.

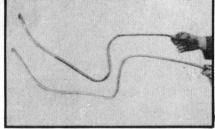

It's a good policy to replace the fuel line, which in any case may have been damaged if it was difficult to extract. Use the original as a template for bending the new pipe.

The original prop-shaft on our car was in first class condition, but very often UJ reconditioning kits are required to restore the health of a high-mileage shaft. If removing yoke, ensure that arrow on yoke sleeve and on shaft align.

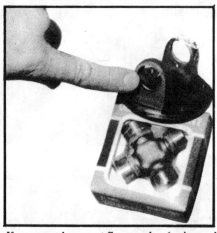

If worn, replacement flange yokes (or journal ends) can be used on Mk 2 MGB shafts (which are the same length for standard or overdrive gearboxes). Unfortunately, if the bearing holes in the shaft are worn, it means a new shaft.

A reconditioned radiator was fitted to our car; this picture shows the difference between Mk 1 and Mk 2 radiators — same fixings are used but top hose connection and filler cap positions vary. The Mk 3 rad. (not shown) is mounted further forward.

The rad. is mounted in a pressed-steel member known as a diaphragm — this should carry a top seal in the groove shown but is very hard to get from BL and sometimes is missing even in contemporary catalogue pictures!

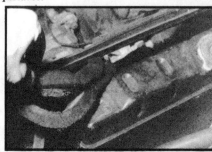

The Mk 2 rad. has an additional soft sponge seal between diaphragm and radiator, though often owners throw it away because it doesn't look 'original'.

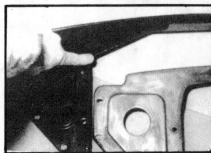

Diaphragm panels vary and Dave stripped and painted the wrong one — even the MGB Centre learnt something this month! Note how shape of internal corners vary (correct Mk 2 item is on right). Hole is for oil cooler piping.

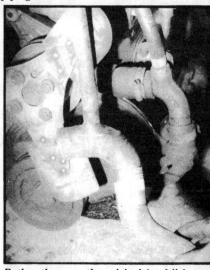

Rather than use the original 'multi' bottom hose assembly, the Centre chose to use the later GRH 498 hose which makes for a neater installation.

It is important to re-fit the oil cooler (we have known owners leave it off). A faulty cooler can't be repaired and the current Serck replacement item (top) is slightly different to the original, though apparently the later item is improved and has a longer life.

It is suggested that all MGB engines are best fitted with the later disposable oil filter cannister (right) instead of the earlier vertical, renewable filter, type — unless originality is more important than convenience to you.

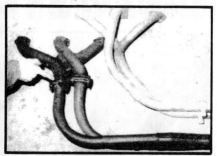

Although not wanting to tune our MGB, when the Centre checked the price of a new cast manifold (the old one had the usual stud problem) it was found to be dearer than the tubular 3-branch extractor type; so that was used instead.

If you are reconditioning the original cast manifold, you will need the six replacement studs and the special 'o' ring gaskets shown here.

Again, as the objective has been to produce a 'standard' MGB, the temptation to fit the larger (1¾ ins) carbs was resisted; but properly tuned and balanced, they can actually result in higher mpg over the 1½ ins SUs.

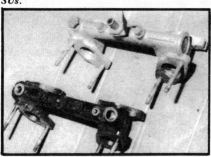

A special manifold is needed for the larger carbs., though these vary even amongst the standard arrangement — here are just two of the many different types.

The engine bay showing the newly-installed tubular manifold, which looks much 'cleaner' than the standard item and doesn't have the six-stud downpipe connection and the attendent risk of an exhaust blow. Spacer blocks on inlet manifold have just been positioned temporarily — heat shield goes first.

Obviously it pays to replace exhaust mountings — this is the front assembly.

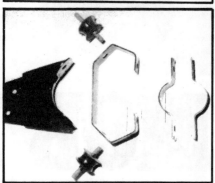

Rear exhaust brackets vary — the earlier, simpler bracket is shown top, and the more complex later set-up below.

The story so far — heat-shield and carbs in place and petrol lines and heater hoses connected up. The first firing of the engine is not far away now.

NEXT MONTH
Re-wiring and painting.

PART 20

MGB Restoration!

Bumpers and seatbelts form the topics for this month's instalment. More from Paul Skilleter and John Hill.

After a brief test-drive just to ensure that all major mechanical components were functioning properly (of which more next issue), our MG roadster was taken to the paint shop. In the meantime, this represented an opportunity to sort out the bumpers, the arrangements for which repay a bit of attention.

We've covered the removal of MGB bumpers before so we won't go over old ground too much — though as John Hill says, it is best to remove the front bumper as an assembly by releasing the bolts which hold the 'L' shaped brackets to the chassis legs, and the one bolt at each end of the blade. Under no circumstances, reminds John, attempt to undo the chrome-headed bolts since without

exception they will round off or turn, as there's no way of gripping the chrome end of the bolt.

Chrome front bumpers are secured by a bolt at each end which passes through a rubber mounting pad and 'U' shaped bracket.

There are two other mountings via 'L' shaped brackets further inboard. On later cars this bracket incorporated a towing eye, replacing the one on the front crossmember as a tow rope fitted to the latter tended to bend the front valance. Pointed out is the half-moon spacer which prevents chrome bolt from drawing bracket onto blade.

MGB Restoration!

To prevent scoring of the chrome, plastic strip goes between over-rider and blade. Still available new, it is worth replacing as the original is usually cut through.

A disadvantage of the original all-chrome over-riders is their susceptibility to denting; the later type has a more practical rubber buffer.

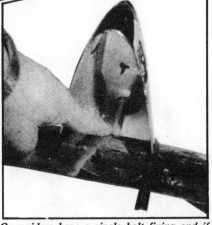

Over-riders have a single bolt fixing and if nudged too hard can swivel round into grille (or rear valance at the back of the car). Shown is the long-bolt fixing for rubber-buffer type — all-chrome ones have separated bracket for bolt (which invariably seizes, incidentally).

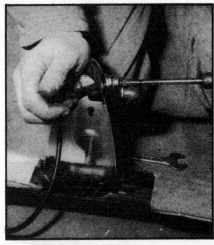

New buffer-type over-rider in place, with the no. plate light assembly being bolted onto it; new light units are available, but the plinth which seats on over-rider is not.

John Hill points out that while all chrome bumpers for the UK market are identical, export-pattern bumpers did vary with different brackets for various market requirements. There were even quarter-bumpers, which few people know existed. This means you need to check any 'new old stock' bumper blades you happen to come across.

Over-riders also varied; originally they were all chrome, then a rubber buffer was mounted to the over-rider which had a flat face to accept it — the different methods of fitting are shown in the pictures. On the rear over-riders, the number plate lights were recessed into the inner sides, except on the very last production models where the front and rear over-riders were identical, with the number plate lights mounted on the bumper itself each side of the number plate.

John also thinks it possible that on the original 1962/63 cars the over-riders were an optional extra, and asks if any historian can shed some light on this. Also, he says, one occasionally sees immaculate MGBs with no over-riders at all, the reason being that of late new ones have been very hard to come by and people have simply discarded their old over-riders and substituted chrome blanking bolts — an installation which is in fact quite neat,

Bolting up the new brackets fitted to our car. It should be noted that the 'L' shaped brackets are handed at the front.

Rear bumpers mount on two apparently over-engineered cast brackets which go direct to the chassis rails between the spring shackle points, but their threaded ends corrode and reduce them to scrap; new ones are available.

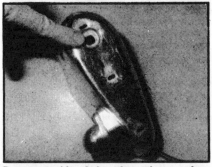

Rear over-rider bolts also seize or shear during removal (all-chrome type), while the long bolt which goes right through rubber buffer-type shown here often revolves in the hole as you try to get the nut undone.

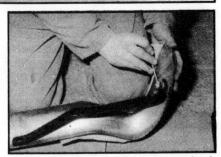

Reassembly of the rear bumper is very simple — just ensure that you have spacers and washers in the right order! Rear bumper irons are not handed.

although one has to make provision at the back for mounting alternative number plate lamps (the rubber-bumper type no. plate, which comes complete with lamps, is ideal for this says John Hill). Incidentally there should be special little brackets to carry the front number plate on chrome-bumper cars, although owners tend to move the plate around and so they do go missing. The proper ones can be seen in the pictures.

Most bumpers and associated parts are available from specialists like John Hill's, though a few parts are currently non-obtainable — like the complete no. plate lamp

MGBs make good towing cars, and if you intend fitting a towbar, try and choose one which does not entail drilling the bumper blade.

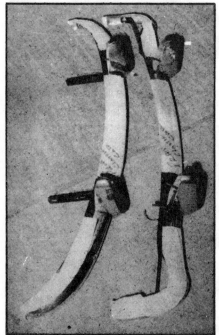

The new front and rear bumper assemblies all ready to go back on our MGB when it returns from the painters.

with plinth for chrome-bumper cars, and the little 'U' brackets for the outer front bumper fixings, but these can usually be found second-hand (reproduction items are bound to be produced in due course). Blades and over-riders are best purchased new, rather than have the old ones re-plated, as it will work out much cheaper that way.

Before the shell went for paint, attention was turned to seat-belts as John wanted to get all welding and other 'heavy' jobs finished before the respray. Intertia reel belts are to be fitted, which meant altering the rear mounting

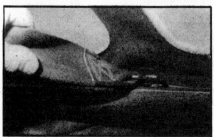

Seatbelts: this picture shows the original top anchorage point for a static belt, where its position so close to the hood leaves no room for an inertia reel. This hole was welded up during the bodywork repairs.

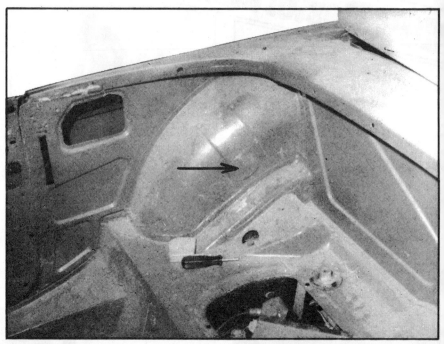

The rear wheel arch of our car, showing a circular pressing (arrowed) obviously intended by the factory to take a mounting point, but never fitted due to production change.

Rear anchoraged points varied widely on MGB's in fact; the MGB Centre decided to mount ours as far back as possible for the convenience of anybody squeezing themselves into the back. A tank cutter was therefore used to cut out a hole in the vertical face of the wheel arch to take the mounting.

as shown — though we would like to emphasise that it is vital that such work is carried out correctly, as the consequences of wrongly positioned or poorly fitted seat belt mountings could be fatal. If you have any doubts about your ability in this respect, get the work done by a competent professional.

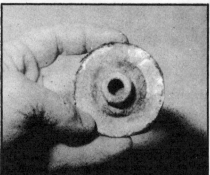

A suitable mounting (a bolt welded to a section of wheelarch) was cut from a scrap shell.

This was inserted into the hole from the inside of the wheelarch, and the overlapping metal MIG-welded from both inside and outside the wheelarch. Note that seat belt mountings are a vital safety point and if you are not an expert welder you should get any relocation of mounting points done by a professional.

NEXT MONTH
Converting to rubber bumpers (not on our car!), road-testing and wiring.

PART 21

MGB Restoration!

Our roadster has a preliminary road test — and we relate how to convert from rubber bumpers to chrome. Paul Skilleter visits John Hill's MG Centre again.

tank, and off the car went on trade-plates for a quick circuit of the trading estate.

Making the 'B' ready for a pre-paint test drive. Steering column is supported by a variety of right-angled brackets in lieu of dashboard; note temporary oil pressure gauge, considered to be the most essential instrument.

This was enough to check that brakes (including the handbrake), steering, gearbox and rear axle were all functioning properly; actually only one fault was discovered, and that was a leaking water-pump. This was promptly replaced — better to remove the radiator at this stage rather than with the final coats of paint on — and then the car was sent to the painters. Incidentally, one item which was thoroughly checked before the 'trial' was the bonnet lock and safety catch, as John didn't want a lot of hard work ruined because someone had inadvertently pulled the cable release prior to the car being driven off.

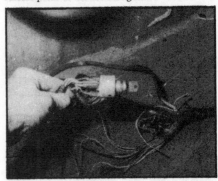

Wiring was tidied-up, all 'live' ends taped, and a ignition switch temporarily added.

As mentioned last month, the car has received its new paint and is currently being fitted-up with lights, dash, seats, trim, hood and all the other fixtures which were removed when the shell was stripped. But prior to visiting the paint shop, John Hill thought it a good idea to jury-rig some essential controls and give the car a quick test-drive, just to ensure that nothing needed attention on the mechanical side which might result in damage to the new paintwork if left until after the sprayer had finished work.

The essential gauges were taken care of as shown in the pictures, and having sorted out the ignition wiring, an ignition key start was temporarily added, as were the rev. counter connections; the ignition circuit was then complete giving electrics for the fuel pump, starter motor and of course the ignition system itself. The remainder of the wiring was carefully checked and insulated to prevent any possibility of lights, wiper motor, heater, leads etc. short-circuiting on the odywork as these components were not yet in position.

The engine itself had, you may remember, been carefully checked-over and fully serviced but not stripped down, as it was in very good order. Sure enough, oil pressure was evident immediately on cranking the engine over on the starter motor (though care was taken not to operate this for too long because they tend to over heat). The choke and throttle were temporarily connected, petrol added to the

Our car is a chrome-bumper model anyway, but John thought it a good idea to cover the job of converting rubber-bumper MGBs to this style because it is at this stage that such a conversion can most easily be carried out — though it is also practical on a fully built-up car.

Removing the original front bumper is simplicity itself, says John. Just disconnect the repeater lamps and then the four bolts holding the assembly to the front mounting plates. Next, remove the radiator grille. Then, using an early-style grille (easily obtainable) as a template to show how much of the original metal has to be removed, the chassis reinforcement extensions are cut away. It is desirable to blank off the ends of these for appearance sake — and if you really want to make a thorough job of it, you can take the extensions right back to the radiator diaphragm (bulkhead) panel.

However, having removed the front bumper you will notice that the front wings

To avoid fitting the water temp. gauge, a blanking plug was fitted to the engine in place of the transmitter unit.

The rubber-bumper assembly removed from the front of a late-model MGB of the type seen in background. Bumper incorporates air intake instead of the car having a separate grille.

(Continued)

and lower valance are different to that of the chrome bumper models, in that the sidelight/indicator lamps are mounted in the front wings themselves on the latter. To convert a rubber-bumper spec. car, you therefore have to either replace the front wings and valance altogether, or if you have the skill and equipment, weld up the holes left in your original panels. As a compromise, John Hill suggests that you at least replace the front valance; this halves the amount of welding necessary, and very often the valance is fairly scruffy anyway (or you could opt for a spoiler which gets you over the problem another way).

If you decide to replace the front wings it makes the job rather more expensive of course, but on the other hand it is simpler to do and John confirms that the chrome-bumper specification wings for both roadster and GT are interchangeable with the rubber-bumper type. Finally, note that rubber-bumper car headlamps have provision for built-in sidelights, and this must be taken into consideration when wiring-up the new side/indicator lamps. The early-type sidelights are available off the shelf.

As for fitting the chrome bumper assembly, all you have to do is make provision in the original front chassis rails to accomodate the two bolts on each of the two 'L' shaped brackets (see last month's episode); the bumper can then be mounted. If you are using an early-type replacement valance, there are two holes punched in it for feeding the bumper brackets through. Note that each end of the bumper is supported by a 'U' shaped

The rubber bumper is carried by a heavy plate welded on top of the original chassis rails on each side of the car. These have to be cut and ground back.

bracket and rubber spacer pad and bolted direct to the valance corners. The front end is now complete with the exception of the paintwork, depending on whether you actually had to weld up the sidelight holes or fitted entire new wings.

The rear rubber bumper is also easy to remove, and you will find revealed two very substantial rectangular brackets welded to the rear valance. These can be utilised for mounting your new bumper irons, by making plates the same size as these reinforcements incorporating provision for a stud of the same diameter as that used on the chrome bumper bracket welded to the new plate.

This plate assembly can then be bolted to the rear valance using the original rubber-bumper mounting holes. The only precaution you should take is to accurately measure the position of the studs — although even here, if you design your brackets with plenty of movement available, adjustments can be made at the fitting stage. When installing the chrome bumper blades, John suggests that you use similar over-riders as on the front (i.e. without number plate lights) so that you can retain the original rubber-bumper type number plate and lamps set-up.

The only tricky piece of bodywork that has to be done at the rear concerns the area directly below the rear lamp. This is flat on

Rear rubber-bumper assembly, with chrome-bumper arrangement on the GT model shown behind. Removal of the rubber bumper is quite easy but you may need help as the assembly is surprisingly heavy.

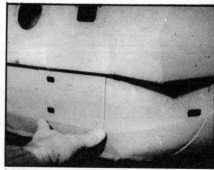

Plate which originally carried the rubber bumper can be utilised for mounting the replacement chrome-bumper assembly.

This area below the rear light should have a curved section added after the conversion.

Rubber-bumper no. plate arrangement; if 'plain' rear over-riders are fitted, this can be retained after the change over to the chrome bumper assembly.

rubber-bumper cars, but curved on the chrome-bumper models. You could leave it, but it is far better to alter it to the earlier style. This can be done by fitting the rear light assemblies, making up the curved section using a chrome-bumper car as a pattern, and welding it into place (it might be possible, of course, to cut the required area from a scrap shell and fit that). Some paintwork is thus inevitable at the rear end too.

In order to complete the job, you need to re-install the aluminium infills (which are available); the next step is usually the lowering of the suspension ride-height, which further improves looks and has a similar affect on the car's handling. Conversion kits for this job are available from the Centre, and we did in fact cover this job in a previous issue of *Practical Classics*.

NEXT MONTH
Fitting-up and re-trimming.

PART 22

MGB Restoration!

This month our roadster gets its windscreen and hood fitted. Paul Skilleter reports from the MGB Centre, Redditch

Heater controls are amongst the items to be replaced before installing the windscreen.

These are the holes through which the windscreen pillar bolts go.

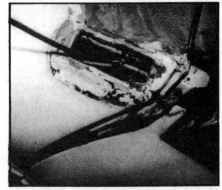

Ensure that the spacer (with one round and one elongated hole) is in position on each side of the car, as pointed out here.

The procedure for refitting a roadster's windscreen differs according to whether you have removed it from a 'running' car (for example to replace the front wings) or whether, as in our case, you are working on a virtually bare bodyshell. In the latter case, there are various items which should be returned to the shell before replacing the screen as they will be difficult or impossible to position afterwards.

Assuming you're starting on a stripped shell fresh from the paintshop therefore, step one is to glue in place the vinyl covering on top of the bulkhead, followed by the demister vent finishers which must be bolted in place. If you intend having an optional tonneau cover later on, also fit the necessary retainers at this point. Next to go in is the windscreen wiper motor complete with cable rack and wheel boxes, up under the bulkhead. Door draught excluders then the padded dash roll follow. Now the wiring loom is fed in (this may be a bit puzzling at first, but you will find it loops back on itself) and located with the cable clamps used originally.

Heater flaps and ventilation closing plates for the demister and interior now are now refitted, but while the dash is not replaced yet, it is essential to feed through and secure to the

The windscreen is fitted as a complete assembly; do up bolts finger-tight at first to avoid breakages.

Check rear wings and tonneau panel for correctly positioned holes, and fit lift-a-dot fasteners, hood retaining sockets etc.

Trimming the rear compartment before hood fitting: carpeting is cut to shape and glued onto bulkheads and wheel arches. Sills have to be carpeted at this stage too.

Tonneau panel finishing strip must be fitted too; it is fastened by 2BA stud plates.

bulkhead the oil sender and water temperature capilliary tube at this stage.

Now you can begin to think about the windscreen. It should be fitted as an assembly (complete with new glass and seals in our case), the pillars locating on the bulkhead structure via slots in the front wings. Depending on the year of the car, either alloy or hard plastic spacers should be in position on the bulkhead side of the windscreen pillars; these are important because they prevent the pillars being pulled too far inwards during the bolting up procedure.

The screen assembly should be jiggled about to seat it on the bulkhead, though it will not assume its correct position until bolted down. There are two pairs of 9/16 ins bolts for each pillar, but screw them up by hand initially because they are easily cross-threaded and will then cause the lower part of the pillar to break off if you try and do them up with a spanner or socket. The screen is finally pulled into position by two 7/16 ins bolts which go into a captive plate at the centre of the screen; again, take great care and make sure the screen remains 'square', doing each bolt up a little at a time. Otherwise there is a real danger of the glass cracking.

Hood and Frame Fitting

This operation (particularly the fitting of the new material) has been covered before in *Practical Classics,* but it won't hurt to run over the procedure again for the benefit of new readers. Assuming you're starting with a bare shell again, here's the sequence of operations.

Check first that the rear wings, if new, are drilled for the studs and locating sockets — some BL wings are, some aren't. Ideally this check should be made early on so you can make the necessary holes before the shell is

Hood frame is offered up to the shell.

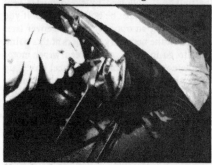

Close-up showing the main hood mounting with its Philips-headed securing screws.

New hood has been stretched over header piece and glued; this is now being screwed to the frame.

The material is draped over the remainder of the frame and the creases pulled out; new BL hoods (and late-model frames) are still available by the way.

The rear hood rail is inserted into retaining plates on top of the tonneau panel.

The hood is seen here being pulled into position so that the Dot fasteners can be attached round the side of the car. The pop studs too can then be positioned (buy new, or drill the old ones off and re-use).

painted. Also ensure that the relevant mounting holes line up with those in the hood frame, and that captive nuts are still in place and have clean threads.

Some of the rear trim needs to be installed before the hood can be fitted, and this is shown in the pictures. The frame can then be attached to the car; ours is the later, 'Michelotti', frame which is easier to manage than the earlier two-part type, or the interim cantilevered one. The hood material is then laid over the frame as in the photographs, complete with header rail which is screwed onto the frame. Pull out the creases and leave alone for half-an-hour or so for the plastic to straighten out a bit; afterwards proceed as in the photographs, the final job being to lower the header rail onto the screen, pull forward and clamp — this can be a two-man job the first time due to the new material.

NEXT MONTH

Dash, instruments and wiring.

PART 23

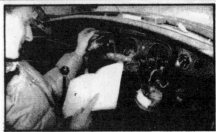

If you haven't one, obtain a manual and make regular reference to the wiring diagram for your car. Don't try to work 'blind'!

Check that the instrument/panel light bulbs work in their holders before finally installing them. When replacing rev-counter and speedo (on all but early cars) note that they both have earth leads — they don't simply earth via their dash mountings.

MGB Restoration!

Hints on wiring and steering wheels this time, as our MGB roadster nears completion. Paul Skilleter reports.

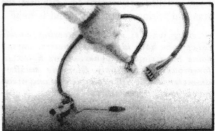

Indicator switch assembly: this had three types of connector, the original bullet type (left), and two kinds of plug-in multi-socket connector on later cars. Don't forget to select the right type of switch assembly for your car, therefore, if you are replacing it.

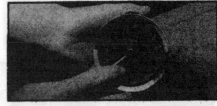

Speedos look the same for all 'B's but are variously calibrated for different gearings; check the last four digets of the number on the face against any replacement instrument.

Calling in at the MGB Centre, Redditch to catch up on the latest progress from John Hill, I could see that the 'B', parked in the forecourt with its red paintwork gleaming, was very nearly ready for the road. In fact, by the time you're reading this, we may well have taken delivery of what amounts to a 'new' roadster; though that will be far from the end of the story as Bob Ashby will then be running the 'B' as his staff car, and reporting on its behaviour.

Meanwhile, it's been a case of completing the detail work — which as anyone who's

First step when commencing to get the electrics working again after a rebuild is to check the fuses. Make sure they are all in position and not blown — and check constantly during the operation as it's easy to blow a fuse when testing, which means you could be searching for an elusive fault when it's just a fuse gone.

Clean all bullet connectors with emery cloth before replacing. If none of the rear electrics work, it probably means the earth lead which attaches at the back of the no. plate bolts has been left off.

Don't rush to fit the headlamp rims back on — adjust the lights first as the rims conceal the screws.

completed a total rebuild will know, seems to take an inordinantly long time; but as we've said before, it's at this stage that what you do is going to show, so care needs to be taken not to spoil much previous effort by shoddy finishing. Also, it's more or less your last chance to ensure that all ancilliary instruments and equipment work properly, and that nothing will work loose, fall off or rattle.

As the pictures show, the MGB Centre has been getting the electrics sorted out over the past week or so, connecting up instruments, switches and lights to the loom which had been installed previously. The 'B' uses the standard wiring colour codes, and is quite a

Steering wheels: all MGB steering wheels except one have identical diameters, though some have slots in spokes, others holes. In foreground is the only BL-made smaller-diameter wheel, still available new and much favoured as a replacement.

simple car to fit up electrically, because it has no complications in the way of electric windows, heater servo motors, or electrically operated oil and water gauges. In fact on three-bearing engine MGBs (1962-1965), even the rev. counter is mechanically driven. However, the detail wiring does of course differ from year to

The hole arrowed on the wheel centre is for the horn plunger on cars where the horn isn't operated by indicator arm. This mechanism looks a bit like a Biro pen and often gets thrown away during dismantling — but as it costs around £6.50 to replace, this is an expensive mistake!

Our 'B' has had its original steering wheel returned to it, and this picture also shows the dash nearly back together.

In the engine bay, the Centre found some channel-section rubber to fit the top of the diaphragm (the original rubber is no longer obtainable); this is an often forgotten item.

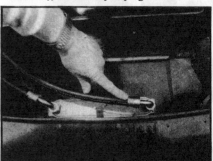

Sharp-eyed MG experts might have noticed the incorrect oil cooler hoses on our MGB at the Bristol Show, quickly fitted just to get the car driveable. These are the correct specification, unequal length hoses in place.

year with MGBs, which why we advise you to always work from a wiring diagram specifically for your model.

Even with a diagram though, it's fair to say that getting everything electrical to work perfectly after a rebuild causes more anguish to many owners than a lot of apparently much bigger jobs, so if you haven't been through it before, prepare yourself for a few hassles. Much can be achieved with common sense and a circuit tester (the screwdriver type which lights up if the circuit works — very cheap from Halfords or similar) however, and if you missed it, our May 1983 issue (still available as a back number) covered electrical fault-finding in detail. □

NEXT MONTH

Interior trim topics — and hopefully, the first proper road-test of the completed car!

On the road again — Bob Ashby drives our rebuilt roadster!

PART 24
MGB Restoration!

After very nearly two years of painstaking restoration work, the *Practical Classics* MGB project car is back on the road. Advertisement manager Bob Ashby has been giving the car a couple of weeks of shake down motoring and, in spite of a short list of things which stuck, broke or just didn't work, he is still enthusiastic.

"Just when my poor old joints had become accustomed to the unusual driving position of the Scimitar, there I was driving an MGB again and all my bones were re-adjusting themselves into a long-forgotten posture.

Not that I really mind, in fact I have been looking forward to running a 'B' again — particularly a roadster — as it has been so many years now since I enjoyed open-air motoring on a regular basis. I re-entered the elements on June 3rd at Redditch when I collected the *Practical Classics* project MGB from John Hill's MGB Centre, where John and his team have devoted as much time as possible over the past two years, covering the rebuild of ARD 916K.

For the first few miles I felt terribly vulnerable, as if every other driver was about to hit me and mess up this nice shiny 'new' car, but old habits soon return and in no time at all I had forgotten the 30,000 Scimitar miles, and was back in my old 'B' again. With the steering and suspension being so new, the car felt heavy and a bit on the firm and bumpy side, but the firmness has begun to ease a little now that I have covered about 500 miles. The roadster is noisier than the GT because of wind noise around the hood, despite the nice new BL hood that John had fitted, but one

Bob Ashby is thoroughly enjoying getting back to "wind in the wig" motoring.

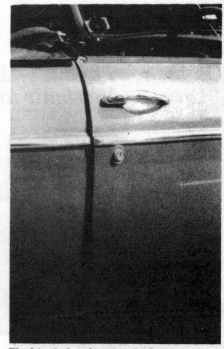

The driver's door does not quite fit.

soon gets used to that and the combination of wind noise, firmness and the familiar MGB exhaust note, remind you that you are in a sports car, and one should not expect limousine comfort.

I had further business to attend to in the Midlands, and needed petrol to do so. The first tankful however, found a couple of leaky unions and formed a rather large deposit of petrol in the driveway of one of the *Practical Classics* advertisers. With his assistance the flow was stemmed by tightening the unions, leaving them to settle and returning again for a further turn from time to time, until it finally stopped. I then had to cover about 200 miles to get home, and although I had only driven the 'B' for about 20 miles so far, and had already encountered a problem, it was a journey that I had to make regardless of what might occur. Armed with my AA membership card, plus my knowledge of MGBs, and sticking to motorways (just in case I needed emergency services), I set off at midnight. I did have one other problem in that my head-lights were not only annoying other motorists, but they forced the Luftwaffe to cancel their planned bombing raid that night.

One or two things are a bit annoying with the car. The choke is stuck, and won't budge either way, the driver's door is not closing properly, the door locks 'don't', there is a blow on the exhaust manifold, and someone fitting instruments has chipped the dashboard. However, the car is a rebuild — not a new car, and as such must suffer from the 'niggly' faults that any reader who rebuilds his car, using the serviceable 'old' parts and adding new items, must also encounter.

The aim with our 'B' was to create a solid reliable and presentable car, not a concours exhibit, and as I gradually rectify the little problems, I get the feeling that ARD 916K will be quite a good and useful car.

Staff Car Sagas will either prove or disprove my feelings. I wonder also how many of the *Practical Classics* readers, hopefully inspired by our project, are fairing with their Bs back on the road.

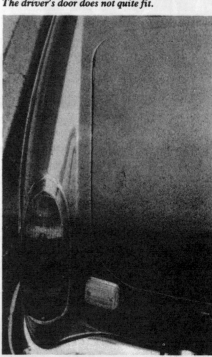

The gap around the bootlid narrows a little at this point.

The idea was quite simple: we'd find a run-down chrome-bumper roadster and with the aid of John Hill's MGB Centre at Redditch, carry out every conceivable job on it (except the rebuilding of the engine and drive train) that a keen owner would be likely to tackle, producing at the end a 'near-new' MGB; and this is exactly what we did do, and some two years later our Group Advertisement Manager Bob Ashby is busy driving up and down the country in an extremely smart roadster which is every bit as good as it looks.

The project started in our September 1981 issue, and in the following months we saw first the bodywork rebuilt using all-new panels, then the steering, suspension and brakes, and finally the wiring and interior brought up to scratch. While it was a stripped shell a high quality re-spray in red was carried out, and new chrome trim was fitted to finally produce a very eye-catching car indeed.

One of the great advantages the MGB has over many other old cars is the sheer availability of new parts for it — there is almost nothing which either BL or the specialists cannot supply new or reconditioned, and the comprehensiveness of the inventory grows each year as more remanufactured goods are commissioned by MG specialists to replace those phased out by BL. This happy state of affairs is due to the numbers of MGBs still in

Ever thought of totally restoring an MGB? We did exactly this with John Hill last year, and now Paul Skilleter adds up all the bills . . .

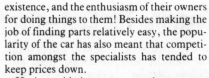

ARD 916K

Counting The Cost – Our MGB Rebuild

existence, and the enthusiasm of their owners for doing things to them! Besides making the job of finding parts relatively easy, the popularity of the car has also meant that competition amongst the specialists has tended to keep prices down.

Having said that, we can only go on to repeat what we always say when it comes to rebuilding cars — unless you own a particularly exotic or valuable machine (and that usually means one that can be sold for upwards of £15,000), a total restoration using mainly new parts cannot be justified on financial grounds alone, particularly if you have to pay for labour in addition to parts. This fact is well worth pointing out to newcomers to old-car restoration — who should always remember that this is primarily a hobby, with the work involved being all part of the fun. If all you want is simply a good or even 'concours' car, it's far cheaper to go out and buy one that somebody else has restored (even if you have to pay interest on a loan).

Getting back to MGBs in particular, another useful aspect of the car is the relative simplicity of the bodyshell, which with the aforementioned availability of panels, makes it one of the most practical cars for the amateur to restore at home. In other words, if you've never renovated a unitary-construction car before, we reckon (having been involved with the rebuilding of umpteen cars over the years) that an MGB is a good bet for a first-time try. In addition to our unique and extensive series of articles, you also have the two MG clubs to join and obtain further advice from, and a wide range of specialists who are also willing to share their knowledge.

Our car was rebuilt in John Hill's workshops by two or three of his staff as a 'background' project, fitted in amongst their more routine tasks, and our thanks to them

This is how our MGB looked during the early stages of the restoration; interior, engine and gearbox were removed before serious work began on the shell.

Counting The Cost – Our MGB Rebuild

for their hard work. Thanks as well to John Hill himself, who broke off from his 'glamour-calendar' photography to take many of the pictures which illustrated our instalments!

Here then, are the actual parts cost of the MGB project, broken down into body, mechanical and exterior/interior trim headings. Points to bear in mind are that some of the prices date back to 1981 when the work began, and that some of these may have altered since. Also, all the specialists have 'special offers' from time to time, which may result in some items being very much cheaper from one particular firm for a period. Overall, however, these listing will give you a very good idea of what it will cost you in parts to thoroughly renovate a chrome-bumper roadster.

Well, the grand total is £3,628.17 if our mathematics are correct. All the parts were new unless stated and some apparent discrepancies in the lists, compared with the

The engine and gearbox were the only major secondhand items retained — false economy really, because both began to fail after a few thousand miles.

actual items shown being fitted to the car, are explained by the fact that some techniques were demonstrated using repair sections, but afterwards complete new panels fitted – for example, door skins were shown being used, but new doors complete were eventually installed in the car.

This total represents more or less what

your parts bill would come to if you took your rusty, worn-out MGB to a specialist and said "rebuild it and use all new parts". But don't forget the labour element — we'd guess some 350-450 hours were put into our car, and if that has to be paid for too, at around £7-£12 an hour depending upon where you go, you will see what we mean when we say that most restorations can't be profit-making operations. On completion, our roadster was worth maybe £3,500 if we were lucky and someone really wanted it; in other words, the parts costs might just have been recovered . . . But even that doesn't always follow.

A further important point to be noted is that the engine, gearbox and rear axle weren't rebuilt, and subsequently the first two have been replaced by Gold Seal units as regular readers will know. BL's Gold Seal exchange scheme is in our view the most economical way of reconditioning your 'B' series engine, because a large amount of new parts are used and you are covered by a proper guarantee. Gold Seal units for the MGB are £356 and

Bodywork

One of the new front wings being fitted, in conjunction with the new bonnet. Front valance was also replaced.

1 pair front wings	£150.00
1 pair doors	£190.00
1 bonnet	£95.00
1 bonnet landing panel	£12.00
1 ditto reinforcement	£2.50
1 oil cooler tray	£21.00
1 ditto support	£8.00
2 mudshields (rear of front wing	£9.00

Here a cross-member repair section is being welded to the new sill floors.

1 bootlid	£85.00
1 front valance	£19.50
2 jacking brackets	£8.00
2 jacking bracket reinforcements	£4.00
2 cross-member repair kits	£6.00
2 outer sills	£20.00
2 inner sills	£14.00
2 chassis castle sections	£29.00
2 front inner wing reinforcement panels	£16.00
2 'mini' front wing mud-shields	£3.50

This picture shows the two rear wing panels being on the car towards the rear of the wheel arch. They both extend up to the body waistline.

1 offside, inner rear wheel arch	£20.00
1 pair rear wing panels (up to body moulding line)	£24.00
1 offside rear wing repair panel (to tail-light)	£15.00

Total for body parts including VAT: **£864.22**

Suspension/brakes/transmission/exhaust

1 fuel tank	£42.00
1 sender, lockring & seal	£15.00
8 fixing nuts	£1.60
1 Borg & Beck clutch assy. complete	£34.50
2 engine mountings	£4.80
2 g/box mounting kits	£5.50
1 starter motor	£65.00

The gearbox mounting on its cross-member represents just some of the perishable components renewed on the car.

1 exhaust manifold	£38.00
1 exhaust system	£28.70
1 set exhaust brackets	£8.50
4 locating plates	£3.00
2 'U' bolts	£5.50
2 damper mount plates	£4.80
2 axle check straps	£5.50
1 oil filter and housing	£7.50
1 top hose	£2.10
1 bottom hose	£4.20
2 heater hoses	£3.50
1 clutch hose	£4.75
1 rear axle flexible pipe	£3.75
2 brake caliper tabs	60p
1 brake master cyl.	£22.50
1 clutch master cyl.	£18.80
2 brake pedal return springs	90p
1 air cleaner connection	£1.00
— engine/gearbox oil	£11.00

Front Suspension

2 exchange king pin assys	£49.00
2 new front dampers	£40.00
2 pairs damper link bushes	£3.20
2 lower distance tubes	£6.00
2 nuts & bolts (lwr distance tubes)	£2.80
4 seal kits	£3.00
2 damper link nut & bolt	£3.80
4 wishbone arms	£28.00
2 front suspension buffers	£8.35
8 inner wishbone bushes	£12.00
1 anti-roll bar	£24.50

The finished interior of the MG; most trim parts were replaced, as was the hood, but the dash is original.

As it is now, our MGB roadster in active service; it now boasts overdrive, incidentally, as advantage was taken during the recent gearbox swap to install one – it makes all the difference on long journeys.

£290 exclusive of VAT for engine and gearbox respectively.

The MGB is now an active and reliable component of our staff fleet, clocking up miles at the rate of 20,000 a year. Just before the winter set in we had the bodywork comprehensively protected by Ziebart's new 'rust eliminator' process, so the car — previously little better than a wreck — is now set to provide many more years of 'classic' motoring.

Note: many of the issues covering the MGB rebuild are available as back-numbers, but a book is in preparation which will be on sale in coming months which includes every instalment — and as such will provide unique source of reference to MGB owners.

2 anti-roll bar bushes and straps	£2.50
2 anti-roll bar links	£17.00

Front suspension was stripped and all wearing parts replaced; here a new spring is positioned during reassembly.

2 front springs	£22.00
1 steering rack exchange	£35.00
2 track rod ends	£8.00
2 brake discs	£24.00
1 set Ferodo pads	£7.00
2 dust covers, disc	£7.00
2 brake flexible hoses	£7.50
Rear Suspension:	
2 springs	£32.00
4 spring pads	£4.00
2 new shock absorbers	£17.00
2 ditto links	£19.00
2 rear shackles	£8.00
8 rear shackle bushes	£2.80
2 rebound buffers	£7.00
2 rebound pedestals	£5.00
2 front eye-bolt & nuts	£2.80

Total for mechanical items including VAT:
£880.51

Trim/accessories/brightware

1 front bumper	£32.00
1 rear bumper	£28.00
2 front over-riders	£29.00
2 rear over-riders	£29.00
2 rear no. plate lamps	£8.00
1 metre bumper filler	£1.50
2 alloy infills for bumper	£4.00
6 bumper bolts, chrome	£4.50
1 set bumper corner brackets	£4.00
2 front dumb-irons	£6.00
1 rear dumb-iron nearside	£4.20
8 bumper spacers	£2.00
1 front no. plate backing	£6.30
2 rear lamps	£49.00
2 reversing lamps	£13.00
2 side/indicator lamp assy	£25.00
2 headlamp pods & wiring	£15.00
2 h/lamp gaskets	£3.98
2 H4 h/lamps assys	£16.50
2 h/lamp rims	£9.50
1 BL hood inc. seals	£95.00
1 hood frame	£48.00
8 studs	£4.00
2 clasps	£6.00
2 backplate/sockets	£2.00
2 hood retainers	£3.50
1 grille assy, inset type	£38.80
1 oil cooler	£24.50
2 oil cooler pipes	£23.00
1 recon. radiator exchange	£56.00
1 windscreen glass & seals	£71.00
2 door cappings	£27.00
1 set trim liners	£38.00
1 9-piece carpet set	£35.00
2 toe-board mats	£18.00
2 sill mats	£9.50
1 boot seal	£8.60
1 bonnet seal	£4.50
1 bonnet/rad. seal	£2.80
2 bonnet buffers	£2.00
2 door Draftex	£8.00
4 Draftex finishers	£8.00
2 sill tread plates	£7.50
1 firewall board	£8.00
1 tonneau rail trim	£3.50
1 ashtray	£5.50

1 set chrome strips	£28.00
1 set moulding clips	£6.00
2 weather strips	£5.50
2 door pulls	£7.00
2 window winder handles	£3.98
2 inertia reel seat belts	£25.00
2 ventilator (¼-light) window assemblies	£88.00
2 ventilator gaskets	£3.50

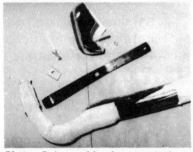

Chrome fittings and bracketry aren't cheap, but new ones make all the difference to a rebuild; replating the original components would probably be even more expensive.

2 rear channel assemblies	£17.00
2 exterior door handles	£16.00
1 car lock set	£16.00
1 boot lock	£2.60
5 Rostyle wheels	£110.00
16 wheelnuts	£20.00
4 Rostyle hub-caps	£10.00
5 Dunlop 165 SR14 tyres	£105.00
2 6-volt batteries	£37.00
2 boot badges	£4.75
2 grille badges	£4.00
— wiring, connectors, terminals etc.	£12.90
2 sets number plates & backing	£14.10
— exterior paint and materials	£218.43
— paint for suspension, axle etc.	£6.00
1 car jack	£12.50
1 tool bag	£5.80.
1 wheel spanner	£3.00

Total for trim/brightware etc. including VAT:
£1883.44

John Hill's LTD.
MGB Centre

10 THOUSAND
MGB OWNERS
–READ ALL ABOUT IT
ALL FOR THE COST OF A STAMP.

Lord Hill of Fleet Street

"The enterprising John Hill obviously considers that us motoring magazines aren't writing enough about him, so he's hit back by publishing his own newspapers. That way he can write all about himself (or rather his businesses) without anything else interfering.

The publications are entitled *MG News* and *Triumph Tribune,* and they're in large newspaper format with plenty of big headlines and pictures.

The idea is really to follow up his MG catalogue so far as *MG News* is concerned, so there are stories about new additions to the range, backed up by hints and tips (how to fold your hood without damage), special offers, and a crossword (I expected more than just one of those from John Hill but there you are). I liked the item about the new chrome MGB bumpers John Hill is able to supply: "…we now have a limited quantity of fronts — the rears are a little behind." Yes, well where else would they be."

Quote From Practical Classics January 1986.

DIY REBUILDS AND RESTORATIONS

Although we wrote the "book" and were shot during the video we haven't taken any work from the professional bodyshops. Instead we have encouraged 'B' owners to tackle their own rebuilds and restorations, lately we have even run our own Body Building Courses. But we still have ideas and new developments to tell you about — so get on our mailing list!

1986 John Hill's Special Edition built from spares.

THE MGB CENTRE
Original

Arthur Street, Redditch, Worcs B98 8JY
Telephone: Redditch 20880

Considering the fact that the *Practical Classics* MGB has been the subject of a complete restoration over the last two years, you may be surprised to find it back in the workshop once again. The reason this time was the engine. Bob Ashby, who uses the MG as his staff car, has not been at all satisfied with the car's performance since it has been back on the road. Although the car has done a fairly high mileage since its restoration, the engine has been burning a great deal of oil and, in most other respects, seems generally worn out – but it was, after all, a secondhand unit .

Obviously a fairly drastic remedy was called for. We then had to choose between the options available. We could either re-condition our existing unit, at great expense in terms of both time and money; buy a used engine from a scrap yard and take the same risk as before; or thirdly, purchase a factory re-conditioned unit, with a full warranty. Not surprisingly, we chose the third option, and promptly ordered a Unipart Gold Seal engine. The practical advantages of this choice appear to outweigh all the alternatives in every respect.

A Heart of Gold for our MGB

Gold Seal earn our stamp of approval, Chris Graham follows an engine swop.

Preparation

There are several practical considerations to be born in mind and they are the kind of simple precautions that make the whole task much easier. One of the most important factors is to find a suitable location in which to do the job. This will ideally be dry, warm, well lit, supplied with electricity and have a suitably hard, clean floor. Then you must ensure that you have all the equipment that you are likely to need. As well as tools, this includes any new parts that will be needed – plugs, fan belt, gaskets, oil and possibly a new set of hoses and Jubilee clips. It would be most unfortunate to reach the stage of assembling the new engine, only to discover that you lack a torque wrench. It is also advisable before starting, to thoroughly clean the engine and its compartment, as it's always much easier to work on a clean subject, with clean tools. Finally, it is a good idea to treat the exhaust manifold bolts with penetrating oil. This treatment will hopefully reduce the risks of festered bolts shearing off.

The process of shutting the car down can now begin with the draining of the liquids. Draining the oil is best done whilst the engine is still warm, thus ensuring a free flow and complete emptying. The water is also best drained at this stage and any antifreeze that the radiator may contain should be collected carefully and stored if so desired. It is not a good idea to spend hours on end rolling on an oil covered floor so, if at all possible, take the car elsewhere to drain the fluids and so avoid the possibility of inconvenient spillage. Next, the electrical system should be shut off, by simply disconnecting the battery. This will isolate the petrol pump, as well as prevent the risk of shorts.

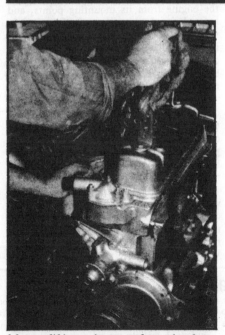

Adequate lifting equipment makes engine changing very much easier especially as careful alignment of the engine and gearbox is essential.

Once the above procedures have been completed, the bonnet can be removed which will provide unrestricted access. However, this job is not as simple as it may sound, and if not done correctly, can result in the bonnet locking shut after its first closing. It is worth bearing in mind that if this does happen, it is most difficult to free it without wrecking the grille. The bonnet should be scribed at the point where the hinge is attached, so that when you come to replace it, lining it up will be easy.

Ancilliaries

The next stage is to prepare the engine for hoisting, and this means the removal of all the ancillaries — carburettors, exhaust manifold, radiator and all pipes and leads etc. There is no established routine when it comes to this stage, it is simply a question of tackling whatever comes to hand first. The twin carburettors can be removed whilst still attached to the throttle cable, or not, and they can be removed as a pair or singly.

When removing the exhaust manifold assembly, great care is needed so as not to stress the pipes in any way. Sections of the exhaust systems on cars that have done in excess of 100,000 miles tend to have hardened up and consequently have become rather brittle. Thus, any undue force applied while removing the assembly can have expensive consequences. Also, the studs which hold the manifold to the block become very corroded and are easily snapped off. It is advisable to remove the distributor at this stage as it is a delicate and expensive piece of equipment. This will prevent it from being knocked during hoisting, but remember to put it somewhere safe and level once it has

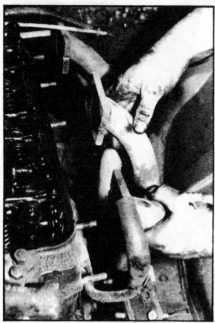

If you put easing oil on the studs and nuts a short time before removal of the manifolds etc. it should make the job easier and help to avoid sheared studs. Do not use undue force when handling the exhaust manifold and smear the studs with Copaslip during reassembly to prevent future seizure.

been removed. The radiator has to be taken out to provide room in which to extract the engine, and once it is out should not just be leaned up against a nearby wall, but placed carefully where it will not be kicked, knocked or scraped. Now remove all the water and oil cooler pipes, and the fan and its belt.

Lifting the engine

The time has now come to get under the car to release the bell housing bolts. However, before tackling this, a jack should be placed beneath the gear box, to prevent any load being put on the input shaft. This is very easily damaged by any twisting movement whilst the engine is being separated. If the gearbox has to come out, it is unnecessary to separate it from the engine. The loosening of the bell housing bolts will also free the starter motor from its mountings, but at this stage, it

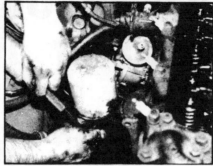

The starter motor was released using a socket extension and ratchet, but the motor could not be taken out at this stage due to lack of space. The starter motor can be retrieved as the engine is removed — do not let it fall on the floor.

is not possible to lift it free, as there is no gap large enough. This means that it has to be left there until the engine is hoisted clear. Do not leave it floundering around in its compartment, lash it securely to a suitably solid anchor on the block.

The engine hoist can now be moved into position and a strong length of chain attached to the lifting eyes. One word of warning here, always check with your manual that the engine lifting eyes are situated in their correct positions, and that they have not been wrongly located. Once the strain has been taken up by the hoist, the engine mounting brackets can be safely undone. Having freed the engine from its mounting points, and before hoisting, it is wise to check once again that all pipes and cables are disconnected, including the earth strap. Now the engine can be raised slightly, along with the gearbox, and eased forward and apart, then hoisted clear.

This now provides a good opportunity to check the engine mounts themselves. Cars of this age often suffer from badly damaged or corroded mountings. They can be effected by prolonged soaking in engine oil, and can be badly damaged by sudden impacts – such as those provided by road accidents.

Once the engine is out, it can be compared with the new unit, and stripped of all the components that need to be re-used. These include the engine mounting and alternator brackets, the breather system and the clutch. With the clutch off, the flywheel becomes

With the engine out of the car other ancillaries could be removed such as the breather system.

Next the clutch cover and centre plates can be removed . . .

. . . revealing the flywheel which should be examined for wear, and the flywheel ring gear should also be checked for damaged or broken teeth. Unless the clutch is almost new it is worth replacing all the clutch components during reassembly.

Gold/Silver Seal — what you get.

Gold and Silver Seal engines differ in two ways. Gold Seal engines are applicable to vehicles up to five years old and contain a higher percentage of new parts. Silver Seal engines apply to vehicles over five years old and the lower percentage of new parts in these engines reflects the much greater availability of fairly good used parts for these slightly older engines. The sole exception to the 'five year old' rule is the MGB for which Gold Seal units are available rather than Silver Seal.

The same standards of re-manufacture apply to both types of engine except that the Silver Seal

specification does not include the water pump, thermostat and thermostat housing and sparking plugs (although plugs are to be included soon), but does include the oil pump and filter and crankshaft pulley. The Gold Seal specification includes all of these items and both types of engine will have been very thoroughly overhauled. This work consists of stripping and thoroughly cleaning all internal parts, followed by close examination for wear, hairline cracks etc. Cylinder heads are checked and tested for compression. Crankshafts and camshafts are measured, reprofiled or reground to the same toler-

ances as a new engine and balanced. [T]he maximum amount of metal which will [be] removed is 0.020″ and any part which cannot [be] reconditioned within this limit will be discard[ed] and replaced, often by a brand new compone[nt]. After assembly every engine is set up, balanc[ed] and "run for thirty minutes under power" ([ac]cording to Unipart) during which time it is subj[ect] to inspection and testing for oil pressure, pow[er] output, smoothness of running and noise leve[l].

I have already referred to the greater availab[il]ity of used parts for slightly older engines and [the] lower percentage of new parts used in Sil[ver]

accessible. This should be checked very carefully for any obvious signs of wear – any gouges on the friction surface, or missing teeth off the ring gear. The removal of the flywheel might pose a few problems, – in that the securing bolts are very shallow. We had to be extra careful to avoid rounding them off. The removal of the flywheel makes way for the back plate, which also has to be removed to be used on the new engine.

Fitting the new engine

That completed the stripping of the old engine, and everything that has been removed from the original engine now has to be re-fitted to the new one. One of the first jobs however, is, to get some oil into the engine. so that it is not forgotten later. Always remember to check that the sump plug is done up tightly.

A new oil seal was fitted to the back plate, this is always advisable when fitting a new engine. Make sure that the back plate fits squarely, but there is no set order in which to do up the bolts. Now replace the locking tag, and the flywheel. The flywheel has to be aligned with two dowels on the end of the crankshaft, and the bolts that fasten it should be tightened using a torque wrench to a pressure of 40 foot pounds.

One problem that can arise at this stage is how to hold the flywheel steady whilst tightening up the bolts. A simple way to overcome this is to wedge the wheel with a suitable hand tool. Also, don't forget to bend over the locking tabs to secure the bolts, then replace the clutch. Make sure that the clutch is correctly centred (borrow or buy a clutch alignment tool for this purpose) and the right way round, otherwise it will not work. Do not tighten the clutch cover bolts consecutively in (say) clockwise order, but work on diagonally opposing bolts in turn so that the final torque is achieved progressively and evenly.

Next, we replaced the brackets – for the alternator and the engine itself, the breather plate and the distributor clamp plate. The unit is now ready to be lowered into the car.

When the engine is removed from a car, there is obviously a considerable loss in weight at the front, and so it rises, usually by about 4 inches. This means that the gearbox drops in relation to the rest of the car, so

before the new engine can be lowered in, the box has to be raised more on the jack, so that the two will line up correctly.

The actual job of fitting the engine into its compartment, and connecting it up to the gearbox, is one that can be done in a minute, or can take an hour. In this particular case, the new engine required a new pilot bush (which supports the engine end of the gearbox input shaft) and this made it an even tighter fit than usual. The problem is getting the engine and gearbox at the same angle, so that they are correctly aligned, and will push together easily.

Extreme care should be taken during this operation, as clutch damage can easily occur if the two are forced together. The engine will not drop correctly into the compartment until it is properly 'married up' with the gearbox, and then both can be lowered in at the same time. Once they are together, and in position, the bell housing bolts (along with the starter motor) can be tightened up, as can the engine mounting bolts. Avoid hitting the bell housing for any reason, as it is liable to crack.

With the engine back in place, the major components can be re-fitted. The manifold assembly went on first – with the new gasket – then the inlet manifold, heat shield, carburettor flange mountings and the carburettors themselves. The vacuum advance retard pipe was fitted next – this leads from the distributor to the inlet manifold. It was decided that the original distributor was in good enough condition to be re-used, although, it did require a new set of points.

Once the distributor had been fitted, the timing had to be re-set, and this was done in the conventional way, according to the manual. The rocker cover was removed, and the crankshaft turned until the number one piston was at top dead centre. This is achieved by noting when both valves on number four are open, and both on number one are closed. The notch on the crankshaft pulley should then be aligned with the correct timing pointer, as specified by the manual. The distributor can now be fitted, and its shaft turned so that the rotor arm points exactly at the number one segment in the distributor cap.

The heat sensor for the temperature gauge

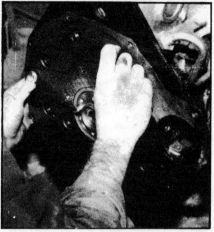

The backplate from the old engine is fitted to the new engine complete with a new oil seal and our car also needed a new pilot bush (arrowed).

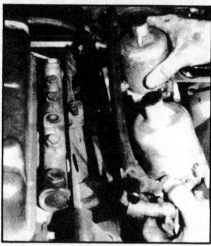

Unless you intend to overhaul the carburettors there is little point in separating them and ours were removed from the old engine and bolted to the new one as a single unit, and we disconnected and subsequently reconnected the throttle cable.

had then to be connected up, and the heater valve replaced. Also, the hot water pipe from the valve to the heater was re-connected. The alternator, a new one to replace the faulty original, was then fitted, along with the fan and its belt. The radiator was the final large component to be replaced, in association with all of its pipes. It then just remained for

al engines. This is not to say that Silver Seal gines are in any sense a second class product. e same standards apply to both types of gine but in achieving those standards several gines may be stripped to provide parts which e capable of being reconditioned for a Silver al engines whereas fewer engines are available from vehicles up to five years old. Unipart ns to offer the same high standard in Silver al replacement engines and gearboxes but to so at a lower cost to the customer. Gold Seal gines come with a 12 month unlimited mileage rranty, with Silver Seal the limits are 12

months or 12,000 miles. Both warranties state that if replacement or repair of the unit becomes necessary due to a manufacturing or material defect the unit will be replaced free of charge and the unexpired part of the original warranty will then apply.

Many *Practical Classics* readers own the Austin, Morris and related cars which Silver Seal engines are already available, and the range of replacement engines is being extended to cover Ford, Vauxhall and Talbot cars. There is some variation in the prices of engines dependent upon the car but we offer the following examples

as a guide: A Gold Seal engine for the MGB costs £356, and Silver Seal engines cost £191 for the Mini 1000, and £209 for the 1275cc Austin Healey Sprite, all of these prices being exclusive of VAT. Further information can be obtained from **Mr S. McGill, Brand Manager, Gold and Silver Seal, Unipart House, Garsington Road, Cowley, OX4 2PG,** telephone **Oxford (0865) 713128.**

The new engine was fitted into the car (clutch fitting and alignment is covered in the text), the bolts around the bell housing secured and the starter motor refitted, then the alternator was fitted, in our case a new one.

When reassembly is finished and you have checked that nothing has been left disconnected remember that you are dealing, in effect, with a new engine and that careful initial use and a period of 'running in' will help to ensure its long life. This article contains some advice on the initial starting procedure and Unipart produce a useful 'Fitting and Care Guide' which gives many recommendations including that the engine should not be allowed to labour or exceed 3000 rpm or 50 mph in top gear for the first 1000 miles.

the oil cooler pipes to be put back on, and for water and antifreeze to be added to the engine.

However, before attempting to start the engine, it is wise to carry out a few simple checks. Drop fresh oil onto the rocker shaft and a small amount down each plug hole. The engine should then be rotated by hand

(without the plugs in, and not by the fan) to enable you to listen for any knocks that might indicate some abnormality. If this can be done successfully, then the next stage is to connect up the electrical system, and turn the engine on the starter motor, until pressure is registered on the oil gauge. This will ensure a complete circulation through all the bearings, without the engine being stressed, and will also prime the oil pump.

The next stage is to connect up the fuel supply, and also to check the throttle return spring, making sure it is not sticking. Then fit a new set of plugs, and connect up their leads. Check that the fuel is getting through, and that there is a spark being generated. The engine is now ready for starting. Remember, do not rev the engine at all. Run it at about 1200 rpm until it is warm, while checking for any leaks, and keeping an eye on the oil pressure. The carburettors, having come off the old engine, will need to be tuned before the engine will run smoothly, and the tappets may well need adjusting.

This stage in an engine's life is the most crucial of all, and so it is essential to conform to the recommended running in procedures regarding rev limits and oil changes etc. Lastly, do not forget to remove, or re-locate, the lifting hooks, otherwise you may end up with a punctured bonnet. □

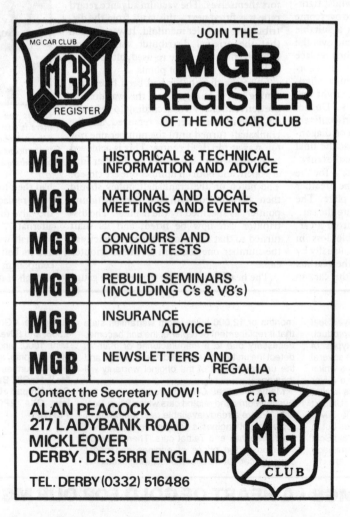

Fitting a New Hood

 There's rather more to fitting a sports car hood than simply slinging a piece of vinyl over a hood frame. In fact, it's quite a difficult job, but should still be within the capabilities of the careful owner, if Lindsay Porter's advice is followed closely.

Having fitted hoods to a Minor and a Frogeye Sprite in the past found watching "Smiling" Steve Langdell, the MGB Centre's captive trimmer, a revelation. He made it look like child's play — and it's not! But you *can* fit most hoods yourself and avoid a nightmare of sags, draughts and flapping vinyl by working carefully and methodically as shown in the following step-by-step instructions.

The first job, and probably the most important one, is to buy the best hood that you can afford. If you can get an original factory hood the advantages are that it is very likely to be much better than those made by outside concerns, it may be better made and it will be constructed of the correct material. The disadvantage of a factory fresh hood is that it is likely to cost a great deal. If you have to buy from one of the hood specialists try, if you can, to avoid buying without seeing first (I have seen some horribly miss-shapen offerings) and get yourself a hood with the clips and stud fastenings already fitted if possible. The small extra cost saves a lot of work — not to mention the risk of getting it wrong!

Do ensure that the hood is (a) the right one for your car, and (b) that it fits, before removing the old one or attempting to alter the new one. The fit can be checked by the simple expedient of draping and smoothing it over the old, erected, hood and checking for shape and size. There will be some useful sized over-laps where the manufacturer has allowed for adjustment during fitting and particularly on double duck or mohair hoods a certain amount may have been allowed for shrinkage likely to occur when the hood is christened by a shower of rain.

OFF WITH THE OLD

When you have assembled all the equipment you need take the hood fabric off. On cars with a folding frame with the frame attached to the cant rail (that section or bar which clamps to the top of the windscreen frame) it will make life easier and prevent debris falling into the interior of the car if the cant rail is detached from the frame as shown in Pic. 2. The cant

Fitting a New Hood

rail, with the hood fabric still attached, can then be removed from the car and the draught excluder rubber removed from its locating channel in the leading edge of the cant rail before drilling out the rivets securing the channel itself. If you have not got a new draught excluder rubber, treat the original with great care.

When all the pop rivets and screws have been removed from the cant rail the glued down fabric can be peeled off and once the cant rail is bare examine its top surface for rust. If there is surface rust clean it off, treat the surface with a rust preventative or killer and then thoroughly paint it with rust preventing paint. If the rust has got a real hold look around for another better cant rail or a new one if one can be found. The MGB rail seems to last well, that on the E-Type Jaguar does not and the rust can cause lumps and bumps below the fabric, rot the cloth backing of the hood and eventually weaken the cant rail.

Once the fabric is removed the cant rail can be re-attached to the main hood frame. We should point out that on the MGB in our pictures the owner had chosen to replace the post-1970 fold-away hood frame with a detachable frame from a pre-1968 car. This unusual "back-dating" was prompted because the Michelotti designed fold away frame takes up all the space behind the seats — the older frame lifts off and can be stowed in the boot.

1

Trimmer, Steve Landell folds down the Michelotti hood frame. The cant rail is the piece on which his left hand is resting . . .

2

. . . and which is easily separated from the frame by the removal of three cross-head screws on each side.

3

After pulling out the draught sealing rubber from its channel, the latter can be removed by drilling off the pop-rivet heads.

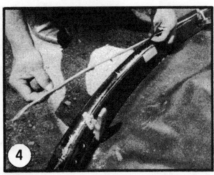

4

The channel is then pulled off its glued base, care being taken not to distort it too much, and carefully stored for later use.

5

The side-window draught strips are folded over and screwed to the ends of the cant rail. The two screws and cup washers should also be stored after removal. Only a coat of Bostik holds the two together now and they must be carefully separated.

If the hood is secured at the back by a flat bar inside the hood and engaging in two slotted clips on the deck behind the cockpit note which way round the bar is *before* removing it from its locating sleeve in the hood just below the rear window. Before you forget, before you do anything else, slide the flat bar into the sleeve in the new hood — ensure that it is the right way round. Pic. 6.

On cars where the base of the hood is tacked to the car a decorative beading will have to be

removed to get at the tacks to free the old hood. Make sure that the wood the hood nails to is sound and that you kill any rust on the adjacent steel. If your car's hood is retained by press studs then you have no such complications to face.

6

The bar which clips into the slots mounted on the rear body panels through the vee shaped gaps (see next to Steve's right thumb) should be removed from the old hood and slipped, right way round, into the new.

FIT THE NEW

With the frame erected, the new hood should be fitted and clipped at the rear and tightly worked into position from the back to the front.

7

With the frame in place and the cant rail replaced the hood must be eased and pulled forwards into its correct position, both from inside and outside the car.

If a hood was bought without clips already fitted, it will be necessary to ensure the correct hood alignment by measuring and marking its centre at the back with tailor's chalk, and to mark the car bodywork by placing a thin strip of masking tape centrally and adjacent to where the hood rests on the body. Then two helpers, one standing either side of the car, should pull and smooth the hood outwards while the positions of two symmetrically placed studs are found by feeling through the hood material and marked with tailor's chalk. These two clips should be fitted (See Pics 17 and 18), followed by one symmetrical pair after another working round towards the doors until they are all in place. All the time this is being done ensure that the back of the hood,

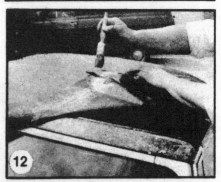

The outer edges should be lifted back up — although probably less than here — and glued back down right to their ends.

Fold the draught excluder strips back into place, penetrate the vinyl with an awl and screw down, remembering to use the cup washers.

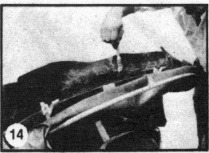

When dry, fold the front of the hood back and glue the vinyl to the front of the cant rail.

Then prevent leaks by gluing down the draught strip channel, remembering to line the holes up with an awl before the glue dries, and pop rivet it back down again. Then refit the draught excluder rubber, carefully easing it into the channel with the aid of a screwdriver.

John Hill helps Steve to measure and mark the centre of the hood so that as it is being fitted it can be aligned to the windscreen centre stabilising rod on the car. On cars where no such rod is fitted, masking tape should be stuck onto the car and a centre line measured and marked onto that.

the rear screen and the draught-strip around the door windows remain taut and smooth.

The centre point procedure also has to be followed where there is no separate cant rail as such, but where the front of the hood has a bar fitted which slots into the top of the windscreen frame. In such cases the fitting of the rear clips is crucial to the fit of the whole hood and it is essential that the *Front* of the hood is fitted before pulling the hood really tight — backwards and outwards. If you want to know *how* tight take a look at Steve Langdell's face in Pic. 11 and if you can enlist some helpers to make sure the tensioning is even it will help considerably.

. . . and apply glue to the cant rail before positioning the forward end of the fabric.

Use tailor's chalk to give yourself an idea of the area to be glued before applying the contact adhesive to the hood . . .

The moment of truth. After lining your marks up, pull the centre of the hood forward hard until it becomes really taut, and make contact between vinyl and cant rail in the centre. Move outwards, pulling forward one side then the other, smoothing the glued joint as you go to give a smooth taut appearance. N.B. "Thixofix" claim that their adhesive is slideable for a number of seconds after contact and until put under pressure — worth a try?

Fitting a New Hood

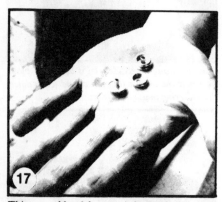

16

Trim along the edge with a sharp craft knife after one final check that it closes tightly — it's too late afterwards if it doesn't!

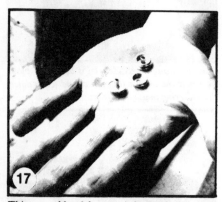

17

This type of hood fastener is known by trimmers as cocks and hens.

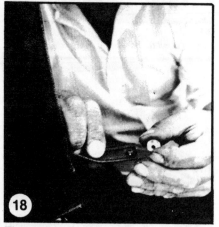

18

The vinyl to be clipped down is marked for position, pierced, the 'cock' pushed through and the 'hen' placed on top.

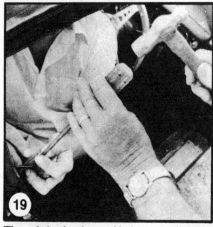

19

The cock is placed on a block, or the face of a large hammer. The tube is spread inside the hen with the end of a cross-point screwdriver, then flattened off with a flat drift. The clip now works as a press stud.

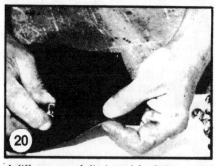

20

A different sort of clip is used for fixing tonneau covers and some hoods at the rear. These are also fitted from both sides of the vinyl. After marking its position a hole is cut using a piece of old brake pipe sharpened with a file at one end and used as a punch.

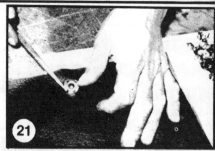

21

Small slits should be cut for the legs which are pushed through the vinyl and the backing plates and bent inwards.

FOUR-SEATER HOODS

Incidentally, the principle behind fitting a hood to a four-seater is just about the same as that of a two-seater except that sometimes, especially on older cars, the hood is pinned to a wooden body mounted rail at the rear and a wooden cant rail at the front. It is still normal practice to fit the rear of the hood first followed by carefully stretching the hood forwards before fixing the front of the hood to the cant rail, but it must be borne in mind that most four-seater's hoods are rather more complex and certainly more cumbersome affairs and so require rather more time spent to ensure a good fit. For that reason a closer examination of the old hood as it comes off and notes jotted down on any of its particularly idiosyncracies will pay dividends when it comes to fitting the new hood properly.

We must stress that this article is intended to assist owners fitting a ready-made hood — there are a number of open classics for which a ready-made, fit-it-yourself hood is not available and this is often because the fitting is considered beyond the scope of the amateur.

MAD DOGS!

Professional trimmers advise anyone fitting a hood to choose a mild, dry day, or, failing that, a reasonably warm garage. Vinyl is affected by temperature and in cold weather you just won't be able to tension the hood correctly — if you fit your hood on a very warm day the vinyl will stretch too easily and the result will be that the hood is dragged and may even be so tight that on a cold wet day the seams will part, or you won't be able to raise the hood and fasten it down.

Fabrics such as double duck or mohair should be fitted dry and will self-tension themselves to some degree once they get wet, but do tension them reasonably well in the first place. Because of the shrinkage factor the makers often leave the hood a little wide — do not try to compensate for this by applying uneven tension at the cant rail.

BMC 'B' SERIES ENGINE OVER~ HAUL

A simple and robust unit which Joss Joselyn believes should cause no problems for the enthusiast.

Whatever may be said about Leyland's ability to spend the taxpayer's cash, there is no doubt that it gets full money's worth out of its engine design. Like its little brother the 'A' series, the 'B', in one form or another, has been used in a great number of different models.

It was Austin's first o.h.v. engine after the war and was used initially in the Devon and Somerset A40. It graduated to the Series III Oxford and the A50 Cambridge in 1489cc form and then went up to 1622cc in the Series VI Oxford and Cambridge.

This was only part of the story, however. It was also used in the ZA Magnette and the MGA, the Riley 1.5, the Wolseley 1500, followed by the Wolseley 15/60 and 16/60, the Riley 4/68 and 4/72.

It was bored out even further and went into the MGB in 1962, but crankshaft problems

led to a re-design incorporating a new crankshaft with five main bearings and the engine survived in that form until the MGB went out of production. In the first part of this article we have looked closely at the overhaul of the three-bearing B-series engine — to be precise a 1,622 c.c. version — and followed up with a special section relating to the five-bearing engine from the MGB.

All these engines are very much alike and we've chosen to cover the 1622 version which was around up till 1962. It still has the three-bearing crankshaft and with manifolding and carburation changes was used right through the range.

The first impression one gains about this engine is that it is totally orthodox, besides being chunkily built and very robust. The inlet and exhaust manifolding, carburation, and the camshaft profiles were also varied according to the application of the engine — with the MG versions being the most powerful. Our friends down at Tipler

engineering, 636 Old Kent Road, London SE15 who overhauled this engine for us told us that it had no inherent weaknesses, although it is prone to wear in the valve train, but generally this occurs only at high mileages.

DISMANTLING

Because all the Tipler engine parts go into an enormous, sophisticated rotary cleaning machine, they don't need to pre-clean their engines before dismantling but it is a sensible first move if you are doing the work at home. Painting it all over with Gunk or something similar and hosing it off is simplest.

Now you'll need a clean and uncluttered area in which to work. Obviously it would be best to have the engine up on the bench but failing this, a clean corner of the workshop would do. You will also need a clean area in which to lay out the bits and pieces. When you start dismantling you may have no idea how many parts will be re-used and need to go back into the same place they were dismantled from. It is therefore far the best idea to have a table or corner of the bench on which to lay everything.

Our photographic sequence starts at this point — with the dirt-encrusted lump of the engine ready to be taken apart. We have not covered stripping off all the ancilliary parts — carburettor, manifolds, petrol pump, distributor and dynamo. These can be taken off on the bench but it may well be found expedient to lift them off while the engine is still in the car. It lightens the load for the hoist and reduces the bulk that has to be manoeuvred out of the engine compartment. Taking the head off before lifting particularly can make a big difference to weight.

It is worth noting at this point that most engine repair operations can be carried out

1 *We start with the engine ancilliaries stripped off and the basic engine lump on the bench. The rocker cover is simply a matter of two nuts and then the four smaller rocker pedestal nuts can be taken off. Head nuts come next and they should be loosened gradually and evenly in the order shown in the diagram below. Then the rocker shaft assembly can be lifted off.*

Cylinder head nut slackening sequence.

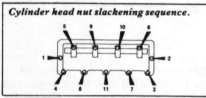

2 *The head should also now be free to move. If it sticks, try rocking it on its studs. If this does not work, tap it all around with a soft-headed hammer, lifting at the same time. Do not try to drive a wedge between head and block — you'll damage something for sure.*

3 *On our engine we took out the studs so it could be completely inverted and the sump removed. If the studs are left in, it's best to do any further dismantling with the engine on its side. Nineteen small bolts and washers free the sump.*

Tools you will need.

Set of A/F spanners or sockets • Engine lifting equipment • Soft faced mallet • Internal and external micrometers • Valve compressor • Valve grinding paste • Valve holder with a sucker • Feeler gauges • Torque wrench • Screwdriver • Complete gasket set • Piston ring clamp or compressor • Circlip pliers.

4 *There's nothing complicated about the remainder of the dismantling. The timing cover is released at the front and the rebuild photographs later will make clear what's involved in removing timing gear, oil pump, etc. Undo the big end bolts, slip the cap off, move the rod clear of the shaft and refit the cap loosely. It can then be pushed out through the top of the bore. Check that numbers are marked on the rods as they are here.*

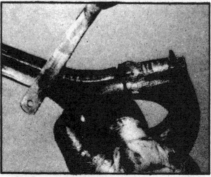

5 *If they are not, use a file or a hacksaw blade to cut small notches to number each one.*

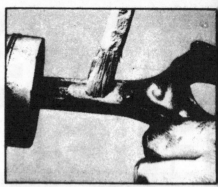

6 *Check whether FRONT is marked on the connecting rods and if it isn't, a blob of paint will help a lot when reassembling.*

without removing the engine. The head can be lifted, the sump can be dropped (after releasing the engine mountings and jacking up) and the pistons and rods can be removed. Timing gears, oil pump and camshaft are also accessible.

The only thing you can't tackle in situ is the crankshaft and its bearings and the flywheel.

If you do decide to take the engine out, you have a choice — it can either be lifted complete with gearbox or the bellhousing bolts can be removed and the engine lifted on its own leaving the transmission behind. The latter is probably the best scheme.

Back to dismantling. It's worth having a series of boxes around in which parts can be stowed and try to keep any washers, nuts and bolts, spacers and any other items associated with the component concerned. It is sometimes also worth making notes — like where the timing cover on this engine has two sizes of bolt and two different lengths as well, and they all have to go back in the right place.

Special tools are not vital but just might become necessary. A slide-hammer device is a good idea for lifting out the big end caps at the front and rear. Alternatively it may be possible to fix something in the centre tapped hole using a stud and nuts and then levering on this.

7 *If you don't recognise what's going on here, it's because it's a special tool (a sort of slide hammer) which is used to lift out the front and rear main-bearing caps. They are a deep, tight fit in cutaways in the crankcase and can stick. In the centre of each there is a tapped hole into which the removal tool is screwed. If the tool is not available, this tapped hole can be utilised by screwing a stud into it, locking a plate on the stud and striking upwards to knock out the cap.*

The front pulley will usually lever off with a couple of stout screwdrivers but a puller, if one is available, will make the job easier. Similarly this can be used to draw off the crankshaft sprocket and camshaft sprocket if they are tight. Take special care of the Woodruff keys in this instance.

Use the reverse order of the nut-tightening sequence in the diagram when removing the head and loosen all the nuts gradually so as not to introduce any strain.

The remainder of the dismantling is all entirely orthodox and once the engine is in bits, it's a matter of cleaning everything first and then inspecting and measuring for wear. Something of what to look for can be seen in the photographs.

CRANKSHAFT WEAR

8 Once the crankshaft is out, the journals must be carefully measured for wear and ovality. There is no substitute for a micrometer and if you cannot tackle it yourself, enlist the aid of your local engine reconditioner.

Any signs of damage on the crankpins or main journals will mean having them ground undersize. The same course will result also from ovality and wear and if either exceeds 0.0015in., regrinding is the answer. Many engine reconditioners insist on grinding any shaft where wear exceeds 0.001in. and some anything more than 0.0005in. (half a thou). Generally however, wear of less than 0.001in. can be disregarded and fitting new shells will solve the problem.

Undersize bearings available are —0.010, —0.020, —0.030 and —0.040in. but the decision about regrinding is generally best left to the expert who will also supply shells to match. He may also offer the alternative of an exchange shaft, which, because it is over the counter, will save a lot of time.

BORE MEASUREMENT

Although it is possible to gain some idea of wear by feeling the depth of the wear ridge on the thrust side at the top of the bores, proper measurement is the only sure guide. Measure diameter under the centre of the ridge and at right angles to it to get an idea of ovality. Repeat the measurements lower down the bore. If any of the dimensions are more than 0.008" different, a rebore is the best answer. Oversize pistons are available for this engine +0.010, +0.020, +0.030 and +0.040 in.

It is best to buy your oversize pistons from the engine reconditioner who does the boring. Availability could be important and he will

9 Similarly proper assessment of bore wear depends on accurate measurement and once again a micrometer is necessary together with knowledge of its use.

bore the engine to suit the pistons he has in stock.

Fitting a new set of rings to the old pistons might be the answer where bore wear is less than 0.005in. A set of oil-control rings might be a still better bet or perhaps a set of PEP pistons specially designed for worn bores.

WORKING ON THE HEAD

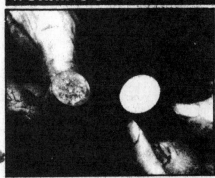

10 Cam followers are easier to assess. If they are pitted like these, they will have to be changed (those from the Marina versions will fit other B-series engines. They are lighter and we found they were cheaper). If they are merely slightly dished, a reconditioner could grind them flat again.

11 Another wear example here, where the rocker has been pivoting on its shaft. Wear of this type is not uncommon on the 'B' Series and a new shaft is a good idea.

Before dismantling the valves, use a rotary wire brush in the electric drill to scour out the inside of the combustion chambers. Leaving them in protects the valve seats. Once this is done, use the valve compressor to squash the springs, extract the collets, lift off springs and

remove valves. The rest of the cleaning-up operation can be completed, including inside the valve porting and the face of the head itself. Keep the valves in order.

Use a rotary wire brush to clean all the deposits off the valves and then inspect them carefully. The inlet valves will almost certainly be re-usable. If the exhaust valves are pitted, burnt or damaged they may need renewal. Pitting, however, can sometimes be tackled by regrinding, work your local garage can probably tackle.

If the seats in the head have been damaged, and they could be pitted or badly hammered, they can probably be cleaned up by re-grinding the seat with a rotary tapered stone or cutter. You can buy one of these for use in the electric drill or get your garage to do the work.

If the seat is too badly damaged for this method to be effective, your local reconditioner will grind out the circle of metal around the valve, fit a new disc into it and then cut a new valve seating. This process is known as fitting an insert.

12 Wear on the oil pump is not obvious, however, and this is how it is checked. Feelers are also inserted between the lobe on the centre rotor and the convex top of the outer rotor. If the measurement for end float shown here exceeds 0.005" the top face of the pump body can be lapped on a sheet of emery cloth laid on plate glass. If lobe clearance exceeds 0.010", fit a new pump.

A new set of valve springs is a good idea, particularly if the old ones have been in use for a few years. Assessing their condition is not easy although comparing their length with a new example will give some indication. Any serious variation from this means renewal.

If the head goes in to the professional for any work at all, it is probably worth while getting him to re-face the head while it's there. This will remove any surface defects and if the head is warped, will restore it level again.

Try the valves in their guides to see if there is any lateral play. If there is, new valve guides should be fitted. The technique for this is to drive out the old ones using suitable drifts and then drive in new ones. Tackle them one at a time, driving out the old one and then fitting the new, using the tops of the existing guides as a level for accurate fitting. It might be as well to have this work done professionally.

Rebuild each valve assembly, ensuring first all the components are clean and then fitting them together with plenty of oil. Use the valve

BMC 'B' SERIES ENGINE OVERHAUL

(Continued)

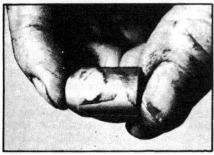

13 *You can easily see the wear on this little item. It's actually the oil pressure release bearing and, if it looks like this, you need a new one. If the spring is shorter than 3", this too needs replacement.*

14 *Valve assemblies are dismantled in the usual way using a suitable valve spring compressor to release the collets.*

compressor in the usual way to insert the collets but make sure also that a new rubber oil control ring is fitted just below the cottor groove.

CLEANING ALL THE BITS

A big bath of paraffin or petrol and an old paintbrush will enable most dirt to be washed off but it is worth paying particular care to the oilways and waterways while the engine is in pieces. Knocking out the core plugs will enable the waterways to be rinsed through and removing the screwed plug in the end of the main oil gallery will help in ensuring this is

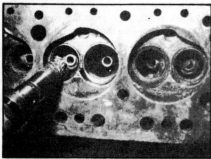

15 *A series of wire brushes in the electric drill should cope quite well with the carbon in the combustion chambers, valve ports, etc; alternatively it can be scraped out and the surface finished off with emery paper.*

16 *Valves are best cleaned up initially on a rotary wire brush and if necessary this can be followed by regrinding, shown here. Your local garage or recon expert will be able to help.*

clear. Use a petrol-soaked pipe-cleaner to probe the oilways clean and afterwards squirt clean oil through them. The whole job is made a lot easier if access is available to compressed air.

This theme of cleanliness must be maintained also during assembly. Up on a clean bench is the best place to do the work but if this is not possible, a corner of the garage floor will do, provided it is covered with something clean — a sheet of hardboard, an old plastic tablecloth or something similar.

If you watch a professional rebuilding an engine, there are always two things he has close by him, a clean rag and a can of clean engine oil. In general terms his routine is to wipe the location, wipe the component being fitted. install it and then oil it or perhaps oil it first, depending on what it is. But both cleanliness and lubrication are vital.

ASSEMBLY

Our photographic sequence and captions highlight the main stages in rebuilding and first of all comes crankshaft installation. Wipe out the main bearing housings in the block with rag; some builders go a little further and wipe them out gently with emery cloth first to remove any burrs or damage. Fit the shells dry, ensuring that the keeps in the back engage with the slots in the housings. Oil liberally and fit the crankshaft into position.

Start out with the standard thrust race and fit the two upper ones first by sliding them round the centre main journal into their recesses, grooved side outwards. Now fit the

17 *Wipe the main bearing housings clean and fit the shell halves, making sure each keep locates in its recess.*

18 *Clean through the oilways in the crankshaft, using a pipe cleaner and forcing oil through to make sure there is no dirt or obstruction. Using compressed air is better still if it is available. Drop the clean shaft into position and insert the upper thrust races, grooved side outwards into the centre bearing.*

19 *Fit the lower thrusts into their recesses in the centre main cap, fit the other half of the bearing and install the cap. Follow this with the front and rear main bearing caps, tapping them home and lining the lower face with the sump flange and the front and rear faces with the crankcase.*

20 *Use a torque wrench to tighten all the main bearing nuts securely down to 70 lb/ft.*

21 *If the pistons are pre-heated by immersing them in hot water, the gudgeon pins can be inserted easily. As can be seen here, the recess in the pin must line up with the little end clamp bolt. It is also important that the FRONT mark on the piston crowns goes towards the front of the engine, that the front of the con rod faces the same direction and the right rod goes into the right cylinder. All this should have been marked when dismantling.*

22 *A quick safety precaution before fitting the shell into the rod — poke a length of thin wire through the oil hole, designed to provide splash lubrication to the bores.*

23 *Always use a ring clamp and hammer handle to insert the pistons without damaging the rings. Note that the block face has been ground flat.*

24 *Big end bolts are torqued down to 35-40 lb/ft and then the lock washer tabs knocked on after the bolt has been moved to present the next flat.*

lower thrust washers into the recesses each side of the centre main bearing cap, lubricate and place in position. Follow this with the front and rear main bearing caps, with their lower shells in place, of course.

With these last two it will be found necessary to hold the shell bearings in place as the bearing caps are tapped down into their recesses in the crankcase. Do this gently and gradually, ensuring that the bottom face is level with the rest of the sump flange and that the front and rear faces respectively are also lined up. Fit the securing nuts and wind them down hand tight. Spin the crankshaft a couple of times to ensure it is still free.

Tighten down the main bearing nuts to 70 lb/ft and once again check that the crankshaft is free to rotate. Now measure the crankshaft end float. This is done by inserting feeler gauges between thrust washer and flange and the amount of movement should be between 0.002 and 0.003in. If it exceeds this, the slack

will have to be taken up by fitting oversized thrusts; if it is too little, it is possible, by carefully grinding the face of the thrust washers on a sheet of emery on plate glass, to increase it to within the required tolerances.

Whether the old pistons are being re-fitted or whether new ones are being installed into a rebored block, the important thing is to get everything the right way round. Piston crowns should be marked FRONT and when they are

25 *We inserted the camshaft next but this can be left if preferred until the engine is turned up the right way again after fitting the sump. Ensure that the lobes don't damage the bearings as they go through.*

26 *Assemble the pump, prime it with oil, fit a new gasket and then tighten the pump in position by torqueing the nuts down to 14 lb/ft.*

27 *Ensure the mating surface is clean on both crankcase and plate and then use gasket cement to position a new gasket, fitting new square-section seals in the end caps (front and back) at the same time.*

28 *Fit the front plate and follow this by the camshaft retaining plate, locking it with its three bolts and washers.*

fitted to their connecting rods, ensure they match the FRONT marking on the rod, whether this is cast or was put on (paint blob) when being dismantled.

It is also important to get the con rods back into the right cylinder — this will be numbered. Provided all this is done, there will be no trouble getting the offsets located properly. What is meant by this can be seen in Photograph No. 4. The offsets on pistons 3 and 4 face each other and so do those on 1 and 2.

If the set of big end bearing shells you have does not have oil holes on every one, it is vital

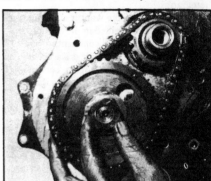

29 *If the timing chain has been supplied with a spring link, join it up. Temporarily fit the two sprockets onto their Woodruff-keyed shafts and line up the two timing dots. Pull the sprockets off again, ensuring the shafts do not move, wrap the chain around the sprockets and refit them, checking as you go that the two dots stay in line. Refit the camshaft sprocket nut, locking it with its tab washer.*

30 *The part of the chain tensioner which will probably need renewal is the pad (on the right). Here it is being assembled with its plate and a new gasket.*

31 *The tensioner is fitted in the compressed position and locked in place by two bolts, secured in turn by a tab washer. Use an Allen key in the end slot to move the tensioner pad (slipper) into contact with the chain. Do not over-tighten, it is about right as shown.*

that those with oil holes are fitted into the rod, not the caps. If there is any problem in fitting the gudgeon pins, heat the pistons by immersing them in hot water and they should slide in easily. Tighten the clamp bolt to 25 lb/ft and ensure the piston pivots easily on its pin. Install pistons and rods as shown in the photographs.

The remainder of the work is shown in the photographs and described in the captions but there are one or two small comments to add.

The camshaft and its bearings are usually in good condition. A good engine conditioner would re-profile the camshaft in any case and if you are in doubt this is a good expedient. Bearings are unlikely to be badly worn. Don't forget to insert the cam followers when the

32 Before doing anything about the front timing cover, turn for a moment to the distributor drive. With the two timing dots lined up, the engine is timed on No. 1 piston on top dead centre. Screw a spare head stud into the drive so you can handle it and then insert it, meshing it with its helical drive on the camshaft, so the slot is lined up at 8 o'clock and 2 o'clock as shown. This will mean first inserting it slightly further round so that when it meshes and turns anti-clockwise, it finishes up in the correct place. Mark the small half of the 'D' to help identification; this is the lower half when positioned (arrow).

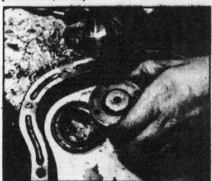

33 Here a new front cover oil seal has been installed and is being driven home using a circular disc as a drift. It must be fitted evenly and without damage. Ensure the oil thrower is fitted (F to the front) before positioning the timing cover. Use cement for the gasket and on the bolt threads: there is a tendency to leak oil. The two long 7/16in. bolts go into the cap and the three short ones into the flange. The remaining four are all ½in.

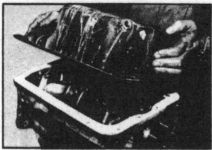

34 As a last check before fitting the sump, make sure the suction pipe and gauze strainer are fitted to the pump. Position the new gasket after ensuring both mating flanges (sump and crankcase) are clean and free from old gasket material. Lower the sump into position and secure with the series of small bolts and washers, tightening carefully to 6 lb/ft.

35 Now, before you turn the engine the right way up, refit the distributor housing, which will also secure the distributor drive, and locate it with its single screw and lockwasher.

36 Fit the new head gasket, using the FRONT and TOP markings to ensure it is the right way round and the right way up. The head can then be carefully lowered onto its studs.

sump is on and the engine turned up the right way again.

The camshaft securing nut might provide a problem. It's ¾in. Whitworth — not a size found in most people's toolkit.

The chain tensioner is not complicated but if you get a replacement that is a pattern part, it may be narrower than the original. This doesn't matter, however.

Before fitting the timing chain cover, make sure you have installed the oil thrower the right way round. The letter 'F' must point outwards; it looks wrong but that's the way it goes.

Check early on to ensure the crankcase oil seal is in the gasket set. It is an item that is sometimes supplied separately.

37 Drop the cam followers into position, lubricating them first. Follow these by the push rods and then the rocker shaft. Oil the shaft liberally and oil each rocker ball and cup seating individually as you ensure they are properly located. Fit all the head nuts and the rocker shaft pedestal nuts and torque them down in the reverse order to that shown in the diagram on Page 36. Head nuts have a torque setting of 45-50 lb/ft and the rocker pedestal nuts, 25 lb/ft.

38 Set the valve clearances to 0.015". This will enable the engine to be started and run but the clearances will have to be reset later at normal engine operating temperature.

39 As a final reassembly job, check all the core plugs and renew any that look at all doubtful, particularly any that are inaccessible when the engine is refitted. Hack the old ones out by driving a screwdriver through, clean the housing thoroughly, coat well with gasket cement and hammer the new core plug home.

On a more general note, never try to re-use old gaskets. Fit the new ones only onto properly cleaned surfaces, ensuring that all old gasket material has been scraped off. Don't make do with time-expired and weakened tab washers. If the one you have is suspect, fit a new one.

When the engine is finally back in the car, don't forget to fit a new oil filter and fill the sump with oil. It is also a good idea while the engine is apart to (at least) clean all the ancilliary items, particularly the carburettor and distributor. □

SPECIAL MGB ENGINE FEATURES

SPECIAL MGB ENGINE FEATURES

Much of what we have said about overhauling the three-bearing crankshaft engines applies to the five-bearing engines — admittedly the block casting and crankshaft are different, but the principles are the same. Overall dimensions were unaltered and if there is a weight difference it is not significant so if originality is not of great concern the five-bearing engine which is sturdier than its predecessors can be used in place of the earlier version. Snags? The engine back-plate is different and the starter was moved, the spigot bearing at the rear of the crankshaft will not match the in-put shaft of the earlier gearboxes, the flywheel is different and there is no provision for a mechanical tachometer (rev-counter) drive take off in the block casting or on the camshaft.

1 The 5-bearing engine is the same in principle to the 3-bearing unit. Here is a 5-bearing crank being lifted from an MGB block.

2 This shows the difference between 5-bearing conrods and pistons (left) and 3-bearing, the latter having a diagonal split and tab-washers — a feature shared with earlier 5-bearing conrods.

3 Unique to the 3-bearing engine is the pinch-bolt gudgeon pin (right) with no circlips.

4 When engine or gearbox swopping, choose backplate, flywheel and starter to suit — early-type backplate and starter shown left, later backplate and pre-engaged starter shown right.

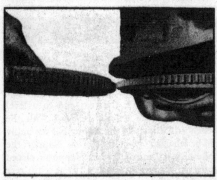

5 Early, thick flywheel shown left, compared with thinner type for pre-engaged starter on right as used on 5-bearing engine.

6 Late-type head in background has slightly more efficient combustion chambers with greater clearance around valves; look for cracks between chambers across the head, caused by loss of coolant.

7 Early 5-bearing engines had long cam follower, later short, altering pushrod lengths. On both the hardened faces can crack. All 3-bearing and some early 5-bearing engines had double valve-springs, later single.

8 Various oil filter assemblies were fitted — vertical upward pointing or disposable cannister type as installed on this Gold Seal MGB engine.

MG versions of the five-bearing engine had an oil-cooler fitted as standard (earlier engines would have benefitted) and it may have become sludged up after high mileages and while you could flush it out you may wish to replace it when overhauling the engine. If rebuilding the engine after a "blow-up", some fragments of chewed metal could lurk in the cooler ready to circulate and ruin the engine once more so the arguments for a new oil cooler are much stronger. □

Our thanks to John Hill of the MGB Centre for additional notes on the 'B' engine. John will be on the MGOC stand at the Collectors Car Bristol Show on 3rd/4th/5th April to answer your MGB questions in person!

First step is to check the condition of the dampers, and the ride height. As shown here, measure the distance between wheel centre and arch.

MGB REAR END REVIVAL

New springs and dampers can do no end of good for a tired car; we visit John Hill and the MGB Centre and find out how to strip the MGB's rear suspension.

It's not too often that something fails badly in the MGB's rear suspension set-up — it's too simple and basic. All you have is a normal Salisbury axle (banjo type prior to 1968) mounted on two leaf spring and controlled by a couple of lever arm dampers. However, in due course, dampers lose their efficiency, springs sag, and even the hypoid in the axle can wear out after extensive mileages. (Or if dirt has got in through careless refilling — or worse still, if the oil leaks out and the axle runs dry because someone forgot to tighten the drain plug).

It is quite easy to detect whether the springs are passed their best — they should have a good convex curve, and if flat or concave, are due for changing or re-setting. You can also measure the ride height by offering up a rule to check the distance between wheel centre and wheel arch. Ineffective dampers are indicated by a poor ride, with the rear end inclined to 'hop' on badly surfaced corners, and their condition can also be checked to a certain extent by pushing down on the rear wing and letting the car bounce back — if the bounce is not checked almost immediately by the dampers, they're on their way out. Also, examine the dampers for oil leaks, another sign of poor condition. A distinct 'clonk' from the rear end is almost always caused by the damper links, not the dampers themselves, though occasionally the blame for this noise can be laid on badly worn splines on wire wheeled cars.

STRIP DOWN

Removing the axle is a surprisingly simple job; you commence by making absolutely sure that the car is securely chocked at the front, after which you can jack the rear end to a level where, when the axle is released with the wheels still attached, the whole axle assembly can be wheeled out below the car. Support the bodyshell on sturdy, secure supports placed under the frame a little way in front of the rear wheels. This leaves the axle, complete with wheels, dangling in space. Before starting to remove the axle the exhaust system, or part of it, must be removed since it passes below the axle tube. Next the prop. shaft is disconnected at the U/J flange and before releasing the U bolts which locate the axle on the rear springs the damper arms, handbrake cable and the flexible brake hose to the axle should be disconnected. If it is intended to retain the brake fluid or, at least, prevent messy spillage, either use a purpose-made clamp to close the hose or place polythene over the brake master cylinder filler and screw down the cap (a less effective method).

Before removing the axle check straps (they may have to be cut off) position a trolley jack below the differential casing to take the weight of the axle. The check straps should be removed at the bodyshell end and not at the axle — the nuts on the lower mountings tend to shear and this awkward behaviour is best tackled when the axle is free of the car and you have more room to manouvre (a little heat can help once the axle is well removed from the car's fuel tank). If the nuts at the upper end of the check strap do not come immediately undone, hacksaw down the side of the nut to remove.

REMOVING THE AXLE

Prior to attempting to undo the U-bolts securing the axle to the springs clean any grime off the threads and squirt penetrating oil around the nuts — sometimes the threads are not very healthy and it is not a bad idea to contemplate fitting new bolts if there are signs of deterioration. Of course, the axle will not fall once the U bolts are released — the MGB rear springs pass below the axle. The axle should be safely supported before removing the springs and the springs themselves are not light-weights so don't take any chances.

The rear shackle assembly can usually be dismantled without much difficulty but the front mounting can be a different story. Tackle the bolt that passes through the rubber bush at the front eye of the springs armed with two hefty ring spanners of the correct size. The nut may be difficult to shift and even once it has been taken off the bolt still has to be slid through the bush and out of the mounting bracket — persistence is a useful virtue, but if

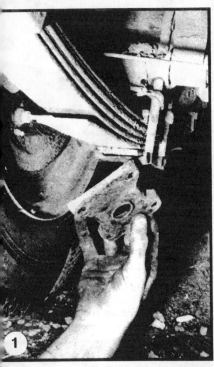

1

Having chocked the car securely, supported the rear end off the ground and used stands or a jack to take the weight of the axle, undo the 'U' bolts and remove the plate. Rear exhaust system has to be removed.

3

The axle check-straps should be unbolted from the shell first; not from the axle. They can be cut with a hack-saw if all else fails. Also visible here is handbrake cable, hydraulic line and damper linkage which must also be disconnected before the axle is free. Links are attached to plates secured by the 'U' bolts.

The free axle can then be wheeled from the car, for replacement or reconditioning. Just changing springs or dampers alone doesn't necessitate removing the axle of course.

2

Free the rear end of the spring by removing the shackle bolts; take care when removing the shackle itself that the spring doesn't drop onto you.

4

To continue with spring removal, take out bolt in rubber-bushed spring 'eye'.

The 'U' bolts can then be placed over the axle and bolted up.

The 'U' bolts in place and bolted up to the spring underneath. Projecting bracket is the pick-up point for the check strap.

Dampers are removed by undoing two bolts — use socket with long extension if possible on wheelarch side (left in picture), and don't remove one bolt before loosening the other.

On reassembly, the springs can be secured at their forward mounting points and the axle lifted onto the spring centres.

Axle and springs assembly all together and ready for installation.

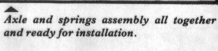

Back axle assembly being jacked into place; some fiddling is usually required at this stage to get the shackles properly lined up and pushed home.

This is the telescopic damper kit for the MGB installed; new top and bottom mounting plates are clearly visible. We haven't tried a car with this set-up but gather that it works very well.

the bolt is completely seized in the bush sleeve cut off the bolt head and the nut and drive out the remainder of the bolt once the spring is removed from the car. Once the springs are removed the axle (still with its wheels on) can be lowered to the ground and wheeled out from below the car. No matter what else you intend to do to the back axle while it is removed do check the brake pipes and ensure that the differential breather is clean — if it becomes blocked the back axle oil tends to fill the brake drums which is not beneficial for the brakes or the diff!

When the springs are removed it is worth examining them carefully unless you have already decided to have new ones. Make quite sure that there are no broken leaves and

remember that springs are always replaced in pairs.

Now we're left with the dampers. These are secured to the car's integral frame by two bolts which if they haven't been disturbed for a long time can object to being removed. It's a help if you can employ an extra-long extension on the socket to clear the wheel arch here, while preventing the bolt from turning by using a ring spanner on the other (damper) side. **Don't** remove one bolt before you've freed the other, because then the whole damper unit tends to turn rather than the second nut undo.

Reassembling the B's rear end is almost simpler than taking it apart, since you will be mainly dealing with newer and cleaner parts. Begin by refitting the front of the spring to the car — and note that to save embarrassment later, the longer part of the spring from the centre goes to the rear! You can then either refit the 'U' bolts to the axle first and then

offer up the spring, or place the axle on the springs and assemble the 'U' bolts around both. With axle secured to spring, the whole assembly is jacked up from the differential housing until, with luck, the rear spring shackles can be lined up and inserted. Note that the detachable piece of the shackle goes on the inside of the spring.

If you are replacing some parts, there are some important differences to note between the Salisbury and 'banjo' axled cars; the 'U' bolts for each are different, and so are the handbrake cables. Additionally, handbrake cable lengths differ between bolt-on and wire wheeled cars, and the chart below indicates the various part nos.

AHH 5227	Banjo axle bolt-on
AHH 5228	Banjo axle wire wheel
AHH 7391	Salisbury axle bolt-on
AHH 7392	Salisbury wire wheel

We haven't yet returned to the subject of dampers, which can of course be renewed without removing the entire axle from the car. If you are keeping the car standard, normal reconditioned or new (expensive!) units can be obtained and refitted, but there is an alternative — telescopic dampers. These are generally more efficient than the older type and last longer too; they are quite inexpensive to buy new and can actually save you money, because the 'teles' do away with the links which have to be used in conjunction with the original dampers. These links wear out quite regularly and cost around £6 to renew, so you save that each side straight away. Both the links for the original dampers and the alternative telescopic dampers vary in length between chrome bumpers and rubber bumper cars, so be sure to order the correct item for your car. An experienced supplier will be able to advise if you are not certain about points like these.

You can obtain a kit to adapt your 'B' to telescopic dampers at a modest cost, and it is simple to fit. It consists of just two heavy brackets, one for the attachment point on the axle, and the other for the new damper's anchorage on the car. The former bracket is held in place under the springs by the axle 'U' bolts, while the latter simply bolts to the car using the holes formerly used by the original damper.

Finally, don't forget to link up handbrake and hydraulic lines, and bleed the brakes. Check straps are best replaced by new ones if deterioration is present, although if the telescopic damper kit is fitted, the straps should be left off as they can cause wheel-lift on corners under certain circumstances. Strap lengths vary between chrome and rubber bumper cars if you intend replacing them. And with all this work completed, you can now go off and enjoy a better 'B'! □

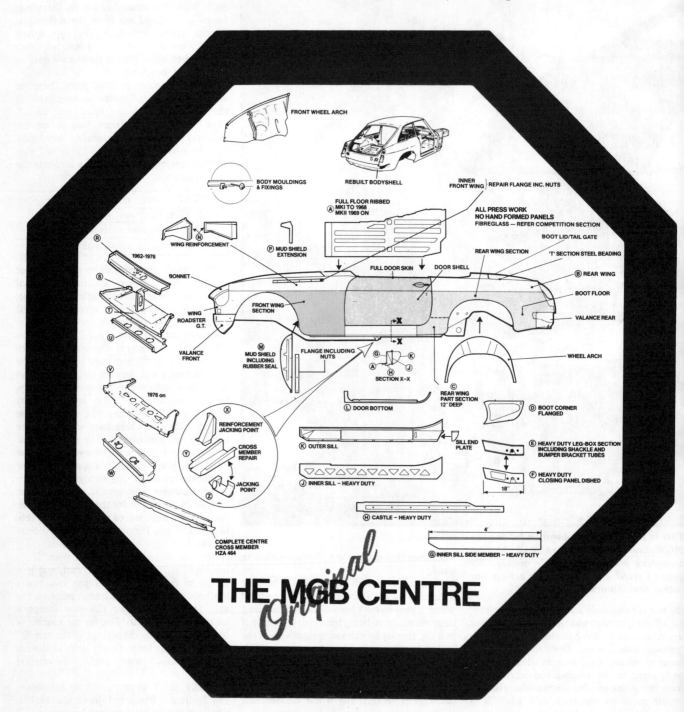

 BRITISH MOTOR INDUSTRY HERITAGE TRUST

BROOKLANDS TECHNICAL BOOKS

Brooklands Technical Books has been formed to supply owners, restorers and professional repairers with official factory literature. The following books are available on Triumph Spitfire/Herald and GT6/Vitesse.

Workshop Manuals

Spitfire Mk. 1/2/3, Herald 1200/1250 & Vitesse	512243
Spitfire IV	545254
Spitfire 1500	AKM4329
GT6 & Vitesse 2-litre	512947

Parts Catalogues

GT6 Mk. 3 (pub. Sept. '73)	520949A
Vitesse 2-litre Mk. 2	517786
Herald 13/60	517056
Herald 'S' saloon supp. no. 2	50873/S2
Spitfire III	51682
Spitfire IV & 1500	RTC9008A
Spitfire 1500 (1975 on)	RTC9818CB

Owners Handbooks

GT6 (pub. '74)	512944
GT6 Mk. 3	545186
Vitesse 6	511236
Herald 13/60 (pub. '75)	545037
Spitfire Mk. 1	511242
Spitfire Mk. 3	545017
Spitfire Mk IV	542220
Spitfire 1500 (pub. '73)	545189/74
Spitfire 1500 (pub. '79)	AKM4544
Spitfire 1500	RTC9221

Competition Preparation Manuals

Spitfire I, II, III, IV & 1500	5th Edit.

 BROOKLANDS BOOKS

Brooklands Books Distribution Ltd.
Holmerise, Seven Hills Road,
Cobham, Surrey KT11 1ES
Tel: Cobham (0932) 65051
Fax: (0932) 68803